Man's Country
More Than a Bathhouse

Owen Keehnen

RATTLING GOOD YARNS
PRESS

Rattling Good Yarns Press
33490 Date Palm Drive 3065
Cathedral City CA 92235
USA
www.rattlinggoodyarns.com

Cover Design: Rattling Good Yarns Press

Library of Congress Control Number: 2023941953
ISBN: 978-1-955826-41-9

First Edition

For All the Men
Who Played
Within These Walls—
And to the Man who
Made it Happen.

Foreword

I wish I could say that I have fond memories of intimate encounters at Man's Country—that I met the love of my life there, that I encountered somebody famous, had the best sex ever, or am still longing for the one that got away.

Sadly, I can't. I only went to Man's Country a handful of times: once to see the Kinsey Sicks, once for a show with a fire eater—can't remember anything else about it—several times to photograph Sarabia's nude dancers, and once when owner, Charles "Chuck" Renslow, gave me a personal tour.

On my first visit there, I was in Chuck's office interviewing him for a book I was writing. "Have you visited Man's Country before?" he asked. I had to admit that, at that point, I hadn't. "I'll show you around," he said.

With that, Chuck took me on a tour of the facilities and explained how the bathhouse and bar next door had changed over the years. Man's Country was a labyrinth of rooms and lockers, a hot, sweaty, separate world—far from the often cruel and homophobic world outside.

In essence, a community center for men. A shelter from the storm.

I so enjoyed reading Owen Keehnen's fascinating book, *Man's Country: More Than a Bathhouse.* It's everything I want from a history book—the factual history and the memories of the guys who sought solace within Man's Country walls.

On a coffee table at my home in Palm Springs, there is a house brick. There's no plaque; it's just a brick. It was taken from Man's Country after it was demolished. Just a little souvenir of a bathhouse that 1000s of gay men passed through and enjoyed.

I want to build a time machine and go back to the mid-1970s...oh the fun and mischief I could have.

St Sukie de la Croix, 2023, Palm Springs, California

Introduction

I began to frequent bathhouses in the early 1980s. Bathhouses were places of dark sexual magic and erotic adventure—gay adult amusement parks that promised sex and delivered on the insular excitement and thrills. Bathhouses were their own worlds.

The first time I entered Man's Country, I could see and feel that it was unlike the other bathhouses I had visited. Man's Country was something more. The unique majesty of Man's Country was more than the sprawl of the place. The layout, clientele, and décor all added to the unique character of the place.

Twenty-five years after being issued my membership card, I collaborated with Tracy Baim for the book, *Leatherman: The Legend of Chuck Renslow*. Chuck was the man behind Kris Studio, the Gold Coast, International Mr. Leather, and the Leather Archives and Museum. Chuck was also the man who created Man's Country. And even more than the Gold Coast or IML or any of his other businesses, Man's Country reflected Chuck.

Working with Chuck so closely for months on that book changed my life. We talked for hours. He was generous with his time, consistently kind, and beyond that, his tales made every minute with him an adventure. It was the best job I ever had. Tracy and I completed the book in six months. The pace was hectic, but both Tracy and I work best against a deadline and we wanted the book ready by IML 2011.

Of all the fascinating topics and stories discussed in my interviews with Chuck, I especially enjoyed researching and talking about Man's Country. Working on that chapter of the book, it was evident that the purpose, pleasures, and freedoms of the bathhouse had changed over the years.

Opening in the days of Gay Liberation when sexual freedom was closely linked with political expression, Man's Country was a safe space, a travel destination, an entertainment spot, a community center, and a place to be a sexual outlaw. It played a significant role in the story of our community and an essential part of thousands of personal histories.

AIDS hijacked the bathhouse narrative. Bathhouses were labeled fuck parlors and hovels of disease. Bathhouses were demonized, with minimal recognition of their importance as places of sexual expression and liberation, of community, and even the arts. Man's Country endured through the darkest days of the AIDS epidemic, adapting by parceling different portions of the sprawl to compensate for the drop in business. A part of Man's Country became the pioneering queer club Bistro Too for several years before the bathhouse was reconfigured, and a different portion then became the leather bar, the Chicago Eagle, before both were reabsorbed into the Man's Country compound.

Chuck Renslow passed away in 2017. Man's Country closed the following year. The building was demolished several months later. Without the physical presence of the building, I was concerned that the rich social and cultural history of the socio-sexual experiment that was Man's Country was at risk of being forgotten.

Man's Country: More Than a Bathhouse is an attempt to capture the personal, cultural, sexual, and social significance of this iconic queerspace, as well as the two bars it housed, Bistro Too and the Chicago Eagle. To capture the richness of the experience, I relied heavily upon the stories and memories of over one hundred employees, members, and entertainers about the bathhouse as well as Bistro Too and the Chicago Eagle.

Through their voices, and with assorted archival materials, *Man's Country: More Than a Bathhouse* is an attempt to not simply be a reservoir for the history of the place, but more a portal onto another time and place. I wanted the book to be an instrument for time travel to the happenings, both good and bad, at Man's Country, and to understand the evolving role it played in gay culture over the forty-five years it was in business.

Welcome to Man's Country

Are you a member?

Room or locker?

Take your towel, your key, and a complimentary condom.

Leave your hang-ups with your wallet in the lockbox and come along

We have a lot to see before checkout time

Chapter One

Rudolph Nureyev ran naked down the halls shouting, "Who wants to swing on a star?" Puppeteer Wayland Flowers held court in the TV lounge in nothing but a towel with his puppet, Madame, on his hand in curlers and a chenille robe. In the Music Hall, a seventy-something Sally Rand entranced the audience with her balloon dance before regaling the towel-clad crowd with tales. Divine performed on the stage here, as did Boy George, Rusty Warren, the Village People, Judy Tenuta, and many others.

Thousands of men explored their erotic nature at Man's Country. Sexual abandon, fulfillment, and education happened throughout this labyrinth of rooms and corridors. Lifetime friendships were formed here, as were romances of five minutes and five decades. Forty-five years of gay history and sexual liberation took place within these walls, and the openness and camaraderie here helped further strengthen Chicago's gay community.

The twenty thousand square foot building that eventually housed Man's Country was constructed in 1910 as Verdandi Hall. Located in Uptown just south of the mostly Swedish neighborhood of Andersonville, the building was the lodge of the Verdandi Society. This Swedish social club had been founded in Chicago in 1880 and was dedicated to preserving the heritage of the Scandinavian people in the United States.

At some point the Verdandi Lodge was divided into several spaces. There were offices, meeting halls, and even a few private apartments. Upper Verdandi Hall, which eventually became the Music Hall at Man's Country, was a popular place for receptions, parties, award ceremonies, ladies' fashion shows, and more.

In 1963, Ingrid and Gosta Bergstrom purchased the building and two years later opened the Verdandi Restaurant and Lounge, billed as the only genuine all-Scandinavian Center in America. In 1969, the Bergstroms added dancing every other Friday.

In this snippet from the 2012 obituary of Ingrid Bergstrom, the importance of the Verdandi Restaurant to the community was made apparent. "With a huge painting of Stockholm behind the bar and a jukebox that played 'Halsa dem da rhemma' and other Swedish songs, the Andersonville restaurant reminded immigrants of their homeland. Nearly every weekend, there was a wedding reception or other event, and once a month, there was Scandinavian dancing that packed the house." ('Grub Street' obituary by Michael Gebert in *New York Magazine*, May 2nd, 2012).

In 1972, Ingrid Bergstrom put the building up for sale. While the building was still up for sale, there was an antique show in the space. At the time, Chuck Renslow and his lover Dom Orejudos, had a mutual friend and lover named David Caldwell. When Caldwell attended the antique show in the former lodge, he took notice of the building. Afterward, he told Chuck that he had just seen the perfect place for a bathhouse.

Mostly to appease Caldwell, Chuck agreed to take a look at the building. At the time, Chuck was the co-owner of Club Baths Chicago at 609 N. LaSalle. He wasn't looking for a bathhouse. Chuck already had plenty on his plate—he and Orejudos were the owners of the legendary leather bar, the Gold Coast, as well as several other Chicago gay businesses.

Chuck and Dom met and fell in love in 1953. At the time, Chuck had a photography business, Kris Studio. He had started the mail-order male-physique photography business the year before. When Chuck first approached Dom at Oak Street Beach, he wanted him to be a model. Dom eventually did a photo shoot for Kris Studio at the Indiana Dunes, but Chuck said they had fallen deeply in love even before the camera started clicking. Soon after, the two men joined forces. Kris Studio became a collaborative effort. Eventually, Kris Studio published gay male physique magazines like *Triumph* and *Mars* and branched out further into early homoerotic film loops.

The pairing of Chuck's photography and Dom's artwork was dynamic, especially when fuelled by love. Dom brought an artist and dancer's eye to the Kris Studio photographs—he composed the photos and posed the models. It was a labor of love. Chuck and Dom were avid fans of physical culture as well as hot trade. Needless to say, the two men had a wonderful time looking for models.

Rather than make him lose his head, love gave Chuck even greater clarity and focus. Chuck was a savvy businessman. Doing gay mail-order business with Kris Studio, Chuck got a sense of the size of the market out there as well as the demand, the sexual hunger, and the money. Chuck never lost sight of that market.

For several years, Chuck organized bodybuilding competitions in the area. Enamored of bodybuilding and bodybuilders, in 1958 Chuck and Dom bought a gym at 22 W. Van Buren. They renamed it the Triumph Gymnasium and Health Studio. During the period when they owned Triumph gym, Chuck and Dom lived in a back equipment room on site.

As Dom described it, "It was the gym in Chicago...all free weights...Sometimes after closing hours we would entertain, and have little orgies up there, it was very adaptive. And then you had the showers right there...It was something like having a playroom...since we lived there it was [easy] entertaining that way." (Justin Spring, *The Secret Historian*, p. 267).

Kris models were given free gym memberships. Word got around, and the men started coming to the gym, providing a steady supply of muscular talent willing to pose. Cash was always a powerful motivator for models who might be willing to do more. Some of the bodybuilders who came to the gym hustled on the side.

During this period, Chuck met gay Samuel Steward, a writer and Loyola professor by day. Sam Steward was also tattoo artist Phil Sparrow. Eventually Steward also wrote several books of gay erotica set in Chicago as Phil Andros.

The trade that pumped iron at the Triumph Gym were Sam Steward's type, and Chuck knew which bodybuilders were willing to make some cash on the side. He helped to hook Steward up. Chuck was adamant, however, that he was not a pimp. "I didn't make a penny. It was the 1950s; I was just helping a friend. All I did was connect him."

Eventually, Steward wanted more. He wanted Chuck.

One of Steward's predilections was chronicling each of his sexual encounters on typed index cards. The cards contained the date and place of the first encounter and was updated with each subsequent tryst. Steward sometimes even included coded statistics that described things like cock size and amount of ejaculate. He kept the typed cards in alphabetical order in a card file.

When Chuck was shown his index card from Steward's Stud File, he declared the card, "bullshit," but never went into specifics.

The address given for the encounter was Phil's Tattoo Joynt, Steward's tattoo parlor in the 100 block of S. State Street in the South Loop. On the card, Steward began listing the journal pages mentioning Chuck, but eventually, with an academic's love of Latin, he simply added, "et passim" (and throughout). Chuck had become an obsession to Steward.

Twenty years Chuck's senior, the possessive Steward fell in love. The attraction was not mutual. Chuck was unaware of Steward's feelings. He liked Steward and had sex with him a couple times, but little more than that. Realizing Chuck did not feel the same, Steward was devastated. Enraged and bitter, he eventually relocated to the Bay Area and set up shop full-time as a tattoo artist there.

If the Stud File card is accurate, Steward actually "introduced" Chuck to S/M in June of 1958. If that is true, "and that was that" seems an underestimation of how quickly Chuck took to it. Either Chuck was humoring Steward and knew exactly what S/M was about, or else his learning curve was phenomenal. In weeks he was organizing a social group of other gay men into rough sex. They met in public once a week. Chuck always said that leather was just the symbol. Leatherwear was how they attracted new members.

Asked about that period, Chuck replied, "We felt maybe if we'd meet in a bar, people would see us, and maybe we'd attract more people who were interested in leather." He said the group first descended upon Omar's Grill. Omar's was a "drag queen bar" in a Loop basement, a cafeteria by day and a bar by night. But the fledging leather group was soon kicked out of that place and every other bar where they met. Eventually, the group developed a big enough following to justify buying the old Gold Coast Show Lounge at Clark and Elm. ("Cool and Collected: For the Love of Leather," Alex Jokay, *The Chicago Reader,* 1995).

In the process of finding a space, Chuck and Dom had created a network of like-minded men seeking hardcore fun, but who also wanted to socialize in an environment where they could be themselves. By the time Chuck and Dom eventually took over the Gold Coast in 1960, they had created a ready clientele.

At the Gold Coast, Chuck and Dom wanted to create a fantasy world of dark sex—an erotically charged atmosphere designed to arouse the rough-sex beast in patrons. Dom's artwork and murals, as Etienne, covered the walls of the Gold Coast. He recreated a seedy back alley, populated with muscled rough types on the prowl for sex. In creating these celebrated murals, Dom was also creating something new and exciting.

"[Etienne] painted the Gold Coast walls re-conceptualizing bars as galleries, beginning the Muralist Movement whose 'Rushmore Four' included Tom of Finland, *Drummer* art director A. Jay, and SoMa's Chuck Arnett." (*The Bay Area Reporter*, Jack Fritscher, 'Who's Your Big Daddy?' 2011).

Dom was a true Renaissance man—a ballet dancer, instructor, and choreographer, as well as a talented musician, businessman, and artist. In addition to his influence as Etienne, Dom created gay erotic art under the pseudonym Stephen, a name he used primarily for gay ink drawings and pencil sketches. Stephen is Etienne in French.

Due in large part to Etienne's erotically charged murals and artwork, the Gold Coast attained an almost iconic status following its opening in 1960.

By 1972, a great deal had changed. In the twelve years since the Gold Coast opened, Stonewall had happened. Gay Liberation had arrived. There were Pride Parades, and chants of *Gay is Good* and *Power to Gay People.* Gay-owned businesses had emerged, eager to tap this ready market.

Although the Gold Coast was doing phenomenal business, Chuck wanted something more, something different than running a bar. The Gold Coast had moved three times in those twelve years. That was a lot of headaches. Chuck was aware of the new market of gay men out there, all sorts of gay men, and all of them horny. The sexual flowering that accompanied Gay Liberation was a golden business opportunity.

Chuck explained it as, "They come to the bar, and they drink, and then they go someplace to fuck." Chuck wanted to have the bar, but he also wanted to own the place where the men went to have sex. He was always looking for ways to expand that opportunity. For the same reason, he eventually owned two peep show arcades near the Gold Coast, the original Machine Shop and the Tool Box. The peeps were a place some gay men went after leaving a bar or for sex instead of a bar. Later, Chuck also had an interest in the gay male hotels that opened near the Gold Coast, like the Barracks and the Crystal Hotel, somewhere near where the men could go and have sex.

Fulfilling the need for gay men to have a place to fuck and netting a profit was the reason Chuck got into the "tubs" business as a primary investor in Club Baths Chicago. Through that partnership, Chuck got a sense of the money involved and the opportunities to be had, but Club Baths was a chain and a fairly standard establishment as the tubs go. Chuck wanted to have the place to fuck, but then he realized that maybe even the place to fuck could be something more.

Trusting his gut, Chuck made an offer shortly after touring the North Clark Street space that was to become Man's Country. To complete the sale, he took on a couple of business partners and sold his shares of Club Baths Chicago. The rest of the money came from the sale of 902 W. Belmont, the building where Renslow's inner circle resided. The Renslow "family," as the group called themselves, had been preparing to move. Earlier that year, Renslow purchased the Dewes Mansion, a twelve thousand square foot Baroque Revival style mansion at 503 W. Wrightwood in Lincoln Park.

In a 2001 interview with St Sukie de la Croix, Chuck explained his involvement with bathhouse entrepreneurs Chuck Fleck and his partner Jim Campbell. "They started the Club Baths chain. Fleck came here to talk to me and said he wanted to open a Club Bath here, which we did. It was at 609 N. LaSalle. It was on the 2nd and 3rd floors. It was RFZ Enterprises, Renslow, Fleck and Zeller. Zeller was Fleck's lover at the time.

"I sold my partnership in Club Baths to Fleck. Actually, what happened was, Fleck came in with me on Man's Country, but he didn't like it. He said it didn't fit the chain image. We were partners 50/50 in Club Baths, so we just traded. I gave him my 50 percent of Club Baths, and he gave me the interest he had in Man's Country.

"Then Man's Country was so successful that Fleck went to New York and opened up another Man's Country there. I had nothing to do with that, that was Chuck Fleck copying me."

Man's Country/New York never had the intent of its Chicago counterpart. Situated over ten floors of a narrow former office building at 28 W. 15th St., between 5th and 6th Avenues, Man's Country/New York was notable mostly in that it could accommodate a lot of men.

"Since I managed the Man's Country here, when I went to New York, they put me up in style and gave me a big double room on the tenth floor," recalled Gary Chichester. "The room was very nice. Man's Country/New York was in a tall narrow building with only one elevator. I was never a fan of stairs, but ten flights is a lot of floors to run around chasing dick. When I was there, they were doing rehab on the place and some of the lumber knocked out the elevator. I didn't think the layout was good for a bathhouse, but back then it was different in that each gay bathhouse had its own sort of style."

Marketed as "ten floors of fantasy," the most distinctive feature of Man's Country/New York was on the eighth floor. Truck Stop was the name of the fantasy area, and it featured a full-sized red tractor-trailer cab of a semi with blinking taillights. The deep and dark cab had a capacity for eighty people and was mostly the site of a continuous orgy. Another fantasy area was a holding cell called Jail Tank. Man's Country/New York also had a wet area with a Jacuzzi. If you were hungry for something other than sex, there was a restaurant inside called the Meet Rack.

Man's Country/New York was a fuck barn that had dollar Tuesdays, attracting mammoth numbers of horny gay men. Though popular, Man's Country/New York never reached the distinctive heights of other New York tubs of the period, like the Continental, St. Marks, or the Everard Baths.

Man's Country/New York is mostly remembered for its iconic double billboard above Greenwich Village Cigars at 7th Avenue and

Christopher Street. The top billboard suggested the Marlboro cigarette ads with a hot cowboy, as well as the familiar font and shade of red. The billboard read, "Come to the Country. Man's Country. Rush! It's just 9 minutes away. 28 W. 15ᵗʰ St."

A second billboard was beneath the first. In the same font, the second billboard had the word 'Come!' in enormous red letters, and beneath it, "to Man's Country."

Man's Country/New York closed in 1983 in the dawning years of the AIDS epidemic.

Chapter Two

Bruce Vilanch shared a great tale on the birth of bathhouse entertainment. "The whole reason that started was because the Continental Baths shared plumbing with a nightclub next door. Well, the landlord could not afford separate plumbing and he could never rent out the nightclub because it was one hundred degrees and humid in there, so he offered the Continental a deal on the extra space. So that's how they started entertainment. It was Bette Midler that really put all that on the map. She played the Continental probably the second week it was open. And the rest is history."

Inspired by the Continental Baths in New York, Chuck wanted to create something special for Chicago as well. The goal was to make Man's Country something spectacular—an entertainment complex, a sex palace, and more. Chuck wanted this to be a place for lovers to meet or explore. He wanted Man's Country to foster the friendships and buddy packs that he saw happening every night at the Gold Coast.

But before that could happen, the building required a complete renovation. The demolition, carpentry, plumbing, and rebuilding were mostly done through connections and by members of the Renslow family of lovers and friends. The renovation also revealed some surprises.

Brackets for mounted slot machines were discovered. However, the Verdandi Club was issued slot machine stamps (to adhere to onsite machines) by the federal government in 1957. A few years later, when it was decided that businesses with slots were no longer allowed to serve alcohol, the Verdandi removed the machines. It was also said that on the lower level, behind a bolted steel door, workers discovered a room with poker tables and a separate staircase for a hasty escape.

During the conversion of the Music Hall, a skeleton was found beneath the stage—but it was the sort used in university classrooms with numbered bones, reinforced joints, and a steel hinge on the jaw. The family nicknamed the skeleton Henry. He ended up residing in the pit of the Gold Coast with a beer in one hand and a cigarette between his teeth.

With Man's Country set to open, the bathhouse was still in need of a general manager. Chuck chose Gary Chichester, who was working at the time as the general manager of the Gold Coast. Gary had worked for Chuck since 1971 and was eager to do something new. "Patrick, my lover at the time, and I, loved to go to the baths," said Chichester. "We went to the Club Baths here all the time and whenever we went on vacation, we were always checking out the bathhouses. We hit them in San Francisco, New York, and LA—so when Chuck told me about opening the bathhouse, I saw it as an exciting career change. I had some definite ideas about things I had seen and liked in other bathhouses and Chuck was very open to listening to ideas."

Man's Country Chicago opened on September 19th, 1973. At the time, the bathhouse was only one floor. Several tenants and businesses in the building still had time remaining on their leases. Renovations on those portions of the structure would have to wait.

In Chicago at the time, bathhouses were legally licensed as "private membership clubs." In order to become a member of one of the baths and purchase a membership, a person had to be invited by a member to join. As a new business, acquiring members this way was a problem, but Chuck came up with a simple solution. He advertised free memberships on opening night—so technically, memberships were not being sold. Hundreds of horny men were there for the opening. Turnout was far above the bathhouse capacity.

"We ended up giving away 700 memberships, starting at membership number 200 and going to member 900," explained Renslow, "and those original members referred people or brought guests." (*Leatherman,* 2011).

"I was member number 211," said the late Richard Johnson. "Right at the beginning of the line. We were all so excited. There were other bathhouses in Chicago. I mean there was one down on LaSalle and Chicago [The Club Baths]. I had gone there and it was nice but nothing special. Locker or room, white towel, porn room, cruising area. This new place was from Chuck Renslow, the guy from The Gold Coast—a hot bar and a hot crowd. We knew Man's Country was going to be something special. We wanted to get in there and play!" (*Leatherman*, 2011).

"I still have my Man's Country card from the week it opened. I have a low number, 1756," recalled the late Chicago AIDS community leader Thom Domkowski. "It really was incredible. The place was absolutely packed. Every room was taken. You could barely move in the hallways." (Jack Rinella interview, 1995).

After the free membership giveaway of opening night, Man's Country charged a nominal registration fee for a free lifetime membership. For every subsequent visit, members were charged only the rental fee for a locker or room.

Renovations on the building continued. By April 1974, the bathhouse consisted of the locker room, a lower level, a steam room, a whirlpool, an orgy room, a TV area, and a small lounge with a juice bar that served snacks. By this point, Man's Country had twenty-six rooms, three of which were double occupancy. There was a room with a round bed, another with bunk beds. Another room featured a St. Andrews cross. The public areas of the bathhouse at that time included a glory hole room, a wrestling room, and a TV room. There were rooms with slings and shackles and more. Though still incomplete, Man's Country was already superior to most tubs of the time. In a promotional color brochure from the time, Man's Country is referred to as, *A New Plateau in Pleasure.*

"Oh, I remember that early orgy room," recalled a member. "It was carpeted, which I never understood! It was a wild room and anything could happen in there."

"Once in that first orgy room, I was getting up from one of those carpeted platforms. It was so dark in there," explained MS. "Anyway, someone came up and gave me the most passionate kiss. I wondered if it was someone I knew because he kissed me with so much passion. By the time I could see, whoever kissed me was gone. I never knew who it was, but that kiss was something I have never forgotten."

"It was a very busy orgy room," added Joe B. "I spent a lot of time in there. I loved walking into it, putting the towel around my neck and just seeing what happened. Sometimes someone would go down on me, sometimes I would sit down on one of those benches and someone would come up and offer me something to snack on."

Once renovation of the second floor was complete, the building capacity reached fifteen hundred. The second floor included additional standard and specialty rooms, a larger orgy room, a glory hole maze, and the crown jewel of Man's Country, the Music Hall.

Man's Country was a place to go with friends after the bars closed. At Man's Country there was companionship, incredible people watching, and now that the curtain was set to rise on the Music Hall, there was entertainment as well.

With the opening of the completed Man's Country in Chicago, the golden age of the bathhouse had arrived in Chicago.

Chapter Three

Chuck chose Wanda Lust as the entertainment and stage director of the Music Hall. Wanda coordinated lights and sound, spun records, handled the talent, and entertained. Wanda had worked for Chuck at his drag venue, Sparrows. Lust was a popular entertainer and hostess around town, performing at the Baton, the House of Landers, and as an emcee and entertainer at numerous community events.

Prior to the opening of the Music Hall at Man's Country, Wanda had emceed and entertained in a makeshift entertainment area on the lower level of the bathhouse near the snack bar. In the temporary lounge there was a stage with a grand piano beside it. The room had white stucco walls and a low drop ceiling with adjustable overhead light canisters. Aside from the piano, there was no furniture. Prime seating was on the twelve oversized throw pillows. If the pillows were taken, seating was on the carpeted floor. The makeshift entertainment area made for a perfectly respectable bathhouse cabaret venue—intimate, tasteful, and perhaps most importantly, it was easily adaptable to orgies.

The grand opening of the Music Hall took place on New Year's Eve, 1974. The affair was listed as "black towel optional" and was by invitation only. Chichester recalled, "We had a cross-section of performers from around town. We sent limos to pick them up. We had the band Gotham and the Bearded Lady and other local celebrities. We had them come in, do a number or two, and send them back to their regular gigs by limo. Doing it that way got a lot of attention. The bars didn't mind. Their businesses got attention and as a bathhouse we weren't in competition with the bars."

Gotham performed several times at Man's Country. "They were fabulous. They were a group of gay chorus boys who got tired of auditioning and put an act together. They did fairly well. And they were all so cute. They crowd loved them."

"Gotham was terrific," added Dean Ogren. "It was so unique to be sitting there in towels. Here's this sex house, and yet you're at a concert. And if something happened, it happened. There was that level of freedom. Where else could you get that kind of open feeling?"

As the resident DJ at Man's Country, Wanda Lust did not simply spin the top hits. Wanda brought a fresh perspective to her duties, consistently giving patrons the unexpected. Wanda had a unique style of juxtaposing sounds and mixing styles. Her classic night mixes, with a coordinated light show, were an unexpected sensation.

Race Bannon recalled classic music night. "Wanda Lust spinning classical music was incredible. Wanda was a genius and the sound system at Man's Country was as good as any disco in town. So I remember those late nights at Man's Country in the Music Hall with gay men lying around the edge of the room in semi-darkness on these big bean bag pillows while this beautiful classical music played. With Wanda spinning it was an ethereal and amazing experience. I remember looking around the room and thinking, this is like paradise."

Wanda Lust was a born artist and performer. Once upon a time in Indiana, Wanda had been a musical prodigy with a specialty in organs and harpsichords. She even chose her drag name in honor of Polish harpsichordist Wanda Landowska. In the control booth, Wanda saw herself as a sort of multisensory conductor. Wanda didn't play records—she transformed the room. Wanda liked to create an atmosphere and then a world. Wanda mixed classical and heavy metal. She played *The Star Spangled Banner* at six in the morning. If Wanda came into the DJ booth and didn't like the song playing, she would drag a needle across the record, and in her booming voice, would announce, "The music is changing, NOW!"

While running the Music Hall at Man's Country, Wanda lived on the second floor of the bathhouse. She usually set herself up in the star dressing room to the side of the stage. The room became Wanda's parlor, where she cavorted and held court for her lovers and admirers.

As the entertainment director, Wanda made sure each of the visiting performers felt welcome. She strove to be a perfect hostess, assuring every act that they would be terrific and then doing everything in her power to make the show its best. During most performances, Wanda Lust introduced the acts before heading to the control booth to orchestrate the lights and sound.

On Valentine's Day in 1975, Bruce Vilanch wrote of Man's Country for *the Chicago Tribune* on the bathhouse's upcoming first anniversary party. "… The evening's festivities will be emceed by Wanda Lust, a 6 foot 4 female impersonator with a rapier wit, a sensational figure, and more red hair than Rhonda Fleming. But the star of the show will be Sally Rand, the 70-year-old fan dancer who was busted four times in one day back in 1933, when she held sway over the Chicago World's Fair. Flatly, refusing to dance with towels, Sally will do her traditional act, the same one Ziegfeld saw. And she will undoubtedly be a triumph."

The piece continued, "What she will not be, however, is the first performer to receive a wet ovation since everybody wears towels, the room tends toward the warm. In the past year, such burgeoning nightclub talents as Judith Cohen, Michael Greer, Marc Allen Trujillo, Frannie, and the sensational Gotham have graced the Man's Country stage. There have also been Mr. Man's Country beauty contests the winner got a round-trip-for-two vacation at Disney World, Man's Country leather fashion shows, and Man's Country "Come as you are" parties, which Wanda Lust says, "are so deeply sick I don't even want to go into it.""

In the September 1975 issue of the *Chicago Gay Crusader*, Fred Alexson wrote about what Man's Country had achieved with offering live entertainment at the baths. "… In New York several years ago, the Continental Baths came into the limelight, not only for its then-unique openness about being a private gay health club but also because it was the first one of its kind to offer legitimate nightclub entertainment to its clientele."

"It proved a more entertaining way for the club members to take a relaxing break from other vitalizing sports activities. Towel-clad young men applauded up-and-coming Barbra Streisand, Bette Midler, and a parade of others who have skyrocketed to success."

"Rising young artists realized that the Continental Baths offered them an opportunity for incredible exposure (no pun intended). Their most common reaction was that "gay audiences were the best kind of audiences to perform to because they are honest and they have taste. If they like you, they let you know it; if you're not good enough to hold their attention, they quietly and politely leave to find other ways of amusing themselves. In the world of design it is no secret that gays are mostly responsible for setting a trend in current styles; they are in tune with the times, and sometimes ahead of them."

Alexson added. "Chicago's Chuck Renslow, an expert in consumer marketing, realized its popularity and potential and decided to enlarge upon it. With the aid of other creative minds, Man's Country soon became another welcomed featured on the Chicago entertainment scene. In one year, the private club's tremendous success has gained it reputable recognition from both the public and the news media (not to mention its members). At a time when many nightclubs and legitimate theaters are struggling to survive, Man's Country has become one of the hottest spots in town for both entertainers and entertainment. Hats off and into the air for Gary Chichester (general manager), Patrick Jordan (public relations director), Wanda Lust (MC), as well as Chuck Renslow and an already long list of entertainers who have crossed the boards of the Man's Country's Music Hall stage—recently including a gal who has graced more stages with her legendary dancing and has managed to wear even less clothing than her audiences here: the illustrious Miss Sally Rand. At age 71, Miss Rand managed to mesmerize audiences with her Fan Dance and Bubble Dance, her bright wit, and her perpetual youthfulness." (*The Chicago Gay Crusader*, 1975).

Rand was booked to play the Music Hall for Valentine's Day, 1974. Rand had starred in silent films and was given her stage name by none other than Cecil B. DeMille. With the advent of talking films, Rand returned to dancing. At the 1933 Chicago World's Fair, Rand performed her feather dance and was arrested three times in a single day for public indecency even though she was never actually naked. As she often said, "the Rand is quicker than the eye."

Wanda maintained that Rand was "definitely nude" for her appearance at Man's Country. Wanda would have known. She applied Rand's body paint. Rand adored the venue. The high ceiling of the Music Hall allowed her the option of doing her balloon dance, though she ended up performing her feather dance instead. Booked into a forty-five-minute time slot, Rand's feather act took approximately seven minutes. Filling the extra time was no problem for Rand. After her dance, she answered questions, and told stories from her silent film days, DeMille, her arrests, and all the cards life had dealt her. Her anecdotes held the crowd spellbound.

That night when Rand was asked how it felt to play to a room full of homosexuals, she replied, "I don't know about that because I haven't seen you fellows having sex, all I know is that there's a room full of half-naked men and they're all admiring and paying attention to me, and at my age what more could I ask for."

Race Bannon recalled seeing Rand perform at Man's Country. "There were two hundred guys in towels watching this tiny seventy-year-old stripper do her fan dance. She was like a goddess to the crowd—she really was. She was wearing these heels and at one point she bent backwards and touched her head to the floor. The boys went nuts. She was having a blast. She clearly loved her gay following."

The first time lesbian bar owner Marge Summit went to Man's Country was to see Sally Rand. "Chuck always made sure I was invited to everything. So I went to the bathhouse to see the show. I guess being there shocked me at first, but I never cared about guy's parts and these guys didn't care about my parts—so I just shrugged it off and enjoyed the show. Sally Rand was so entertaining. And let me tell you, she had a hell of a body. Sally Rand was hot."

"I had heard my father and my grandfather talk about Sally Rand," said Dean Ogren. "I loved her. She was a long-time performer who had lived this incredible life. She had great stories. She said all she had wanted to do in life was celebrate dance and happiness and the human form. I remember listening to her and thinking about all she had gone through because of that—and she was happy. Her message was about saying to hell with everyone else and just being who you are."

After the success of the Sally Rand show, the Music Hall stage was declared officially open. Many of the performers played Man's Country as well as other gay bathhouses and nightclubs in what was affectionately referred to as "the KY Circuit." Performing on that circuit meant that playing to a half-naked crowd was part of the gig. If the crowd got frisky, the show continued. Most performers with any amount of time on the circuit had seen just about everything.

Talent was not booked from an outside source, but by the management of Man's Country. "A lot of it was word of mouth, people recommending people," said manager Gary Chichester. "One of the best parts of that job was being a talent scout. We would read about acts in *After Dark* and went to see different performers in New York. And then, once we started booking acts, the acts started to seek us out."

In addition to booking the acts, Chichester explained the scheduling of performers. "If it was a national act like Wayland Flowers or Charles Pierce or Rusty Warren, we tried to book them for four days, Wednesday through Saturday nights. That was about once a month. On the other Wednesdays, we would feature more local talent."

Gay ventriloquist Wayland Flowers (1939-1988) and his puppet Madame played the stage at Man's Country. "Wayland was a very shy man," recalled Chichester. "Then he would get on stage for the sound check with Madame on his hand and she would come out. Madame actually did the sound check and lighting cues. Wayland was also one of the only acts who wanted to stay at Man's Country rather than at a hotel." Flowers liked to cruise the halls with a towel around his waist and Madame on his hand. "And after his show," added Chichester, "I went to the TV room and there was Wayland with Madame on his arm in a chenille bathrobe with her hair in curlers. And Madame was holding court and talking away."

Another act to play the stage at Man's Country was Betty Rhodes (1935-1987). A veteran of the original production of *Jacques Brel is Alive and Well and Living in Paris*, Rhodes brought good old-fashioned New York cabaret to the Music Hall.

Bette Davis did not play the Music Hall at Man's Country, but Charles Pierce did. Pierce (1926-1999) was a mistress of surprise and disguise. Pierce was a gay legend of the time—known coast to coast for his campy impersonations of Davis, Tallulah Bankhead, Mae West, Joan Crawford, and more.

In 1975, the *Chicago Gay Crusader* piece, Fred Alexson covered a couple acts that were playing at the Music Hall. "CC Ford and Jade and Sarsaparilla, two female musical duo acts, demonstrate how two people of the same sex can translate human emotions on every level with an understanding [of] intimacy through song. This is communication that comes from the spirit and a beautiful experience for everyone to share. When you're communicating love, it doesn't matter how you express it, as long as you express it."

Alexson continued, "Jade and Sarsaparilla recently made their national TV debut on the Music Hall stage in an ABC Wide World of Entertainment Special entitled, *Homosexuals Out of the Shadows*, produced by Joe Decola. The ABC film crew enthusiastically spent hours taping not only the performances but also all the other aspects of the club's facilities." (Fred Alexson, *Chicago Gay Crusader*, September 1975).

Bruce Vilanch played the Music Hall as well as reported on it. "Chuck Renslow saw me at Punchinellos. At the time I would get up and do News of the Day commentary. Chuck asked if I wanted to play Man's Country. It was the first time I ever performed for an exclusively male audience. I did several musical parodies and my topical stuff. Also, because of the work I did for the *Chicago Tribune* I had a lot of celebrity stories. I told stories about Joan Crawford and Ann Landers that kept their attention."

Vilanch also performed at Man's Country with pianist Bruce Robbins. The pairing was billed as Bruce & Bruce. Billed as "America's Most Exciting Pianist" and an entertainer, a man the *Chicago Tribune* said, "performed in the style of Liberace," Bruce Robins played Man's Country as a solo act. He also was accompanist for several vocalists who performed there. Robbins died of hepatitis in 1993.

Aliotta Haynes Jeremiah, the rock trio behind the 1972 regional hit *Lake Shore Drive,* also played the Music Hall stage. A classic for many Chicagoans, the song was on their 1973 album and contained the popular refrain:

> *And there ain't no road just like it*
> *Anywhere I found*
> *Running south on Lake Shore Drive heading into town*
> *Just slippin' on by on LSD, Friday night trouble bound.*

Holly Woodlawn (1946-2015) brought her cabaret act to Man's Country. Woodlawn was a trans Puerto Rican actress and Warhol superstar praised by Bette Davis for her performance in *Trash* (1970). George Cukor petitioned to have her nominated for Best Actress. Woodlawn was also the "Holly came from Miami F-L-A..." in Lou Reed's rock classic, *Walk on the Wild Side*. At Man's Country, Holly sang songs and told some of her stories.

The Kinsey Sicks graced the Music Hall stage with their song parodies and witty original compositions. The colorful and high-energy group was billed as "America's Favorite Dragapella Beauty Shop Quartet."

A staff member suggested booking the duo of Jacober and Oman after seeing them play at the Buttery in the Ambassador East, and the act was booked. The male/female duo brought their popular light rock and rhythm sound to the Music Hall.

The evening that Liz Torres played Man's Country, Rick Karlin was in attendance. "Torres was a New York comic and cabaret singer. A voluptuous Latina with a great singing voice." Torres worked consistently in clubs, on television, and stage. Torres also replaced Rita Moreno in the Broadway bathhouse hit, *The Ritz*.

Chicago singer-songwriter Franne Golde performed at Man's Country several times. Golde was extremely popular. "Her manager wanted her to be the new Bette Midler," recalled Gary Chichester. "Franne was signed with Atlantic Records at the time. Franne had a terrific voice. Once when she was at Man's Country, her manager had a thirty-member gospel choir backing her. I don't know how he managed to swing having them come in to sing backup on one song." In the years since, Golde has found enormous success as a songwriter.

Larry Paulette starred in the original off-Broadway production *Let My People Come: A Sexual Musical*, which ran from 1974 to 1976. In the production, Paulette brought down the house night after night singing, 'I'm Gay.' Billed as "the gay volcano of song," Paulette came to Man's Country in 1977 to promote his album, *What Makes a Man a Man*. The Vanguard Records release was one of the first openly gay albums released by a major label. For his performance at Man's Country, Paulette brought along his backup singers, the Swishblades.

Warhol actress, Bowie muse, rock singer, and poet Cherry Vanilla played the Man's Country Music Hall. Vanilla wrote of her Man's Country experience in her 2010 memoir, *Lick Me: How I Became Cherry Vanilla*: "I made my entrance in an airline stewardess getup, singing, 'Hi fairies, I want to fly with you'—which, thank God, was taken in the right spirit."

Impressionist and comic Daphne David played Man's Country. The daytime talk show veteran came to the Music Hall stage "with all her wigs to transition into your favorite stars." Her repertoire included Katherine Hepburn, Gloria Swanson, Marlene Dietrich, Carmen Miranda, and Joel Grey in *Cabaret*.

Comic Michael Greer (1943-2002) performed on the Man's Country stage. Greer was best known for his role as Queenie in the early gay film, *Fortune and Men's Eyes* (1971) as well as *The Gay Deceivers* (1969), and later *The Rose* (1979). When Greer appeared at Man's Country, he did his "well-hung Mona Lisa" routine. In the bit, Greer dressed as Mona Lisa, giving wry observations as the iconic muse while standing behind a large picture frame.

Magician and "master of levitation" Barclay Shaw came to Man's Country and brought his puppets as well—Madame Cluck, "the world's foulest chicken." Chichester shared that "Shaw was trying out his act at Man's Country. He was on his way to Las Vegas." Shaw went on to become a draw on the strip for years, even touring with Liberace for a while. Shaw died in 1992.

Walter Anthony was another magician who played the Music Hall. In a 1985 Rick Kogan piece in *Chicago Tribune*, Anthony explained that he wasn't the best magician—instead, he had something extra. "I do a very splashy show," he says. "I use a lot of humor, a lot of interplay with the audience and, of course, one miraculous thing every five minutes." (*Chicago Tribune*, 'There's Magic When Anthony Takes the Floor,' June 28, 1985).

Insult comic extraordinaire, Pudgy (1946-2007), performed at Man's Country on more than one occasion. A Chicago area native, Pudgy (Beverly Wines), was a blistering combination of Totie Fields and Don Rickles. And she could sing. Pudgy died on Christmas in 2007 in Las Vegas. In her *Windy City Times* obituary, Chichester said, "Pudgy has always been a friend of Chicago's gay community. From her start as a waitress at the late-night showbiz hangout Punchinello's on Rush to her performance at the first International Mr. Leather, she was always involved with the community both in Chicago and her newfound home in Las Vegas. She will be greatly missed; she was a one-of-a-kind talent."

One of Pudgy's frequent gigs was to emcee the annual Mr. Man's Country contest held at the bathhouse. Joey McDonald shared his story of competing in 1981. "First of all, I was talked into it. The night before I hurt my throat playing with someone very well endowed. Backstage, I told Pudgy I couldn't really talk because of my throat. I was so skinny at the time. That night I wore electric blue cowboy boots with red heels and had a rawhide string around my neck. Since I said I couldn't talk, Pudgy immediately walked over to me. 'Contestant #4 can't speak too well this evening.' Pudgy then asked how I hurt my throat and put the microphone in front of me. So, I showed her how I hurt my throat, by trying to put the microphone in my mouth. Pudgy just gave me a look and said, 'Trash!'"

Theatrical groups, dance companies, a choir, acrobats, and jugglers also played the well-worn stage of the Music Hall. There was a hypnotist who had a couple members running back and forth to the bathroom, desperate to pee and then forgetting why they were there. Another member was hypnotized to believe that he was Dolly Parton and promptly started to belt out "9 to 5."

Bawdy comic legend Rusty 'Knockers Up' Warren (1931-2021) also played the Music Hall. In a 2010 interview, Warren recalled: "It was Phyllis Diller who convinced me to play Man's Country. She said you gotta do it. Well, it meant restructuring my show a little since my act was mostly sort of male/female jokes and funnies—but when it comes down to it, relationships are relationships.

"Anyway, so I get there and all the men were in towels—for the most part well-behaved. There was me, my drummer, piano player Bruce Robbins, my valet, and my road manager Eva. That was my entourage. So anyway, I started my act and there was one guy on a riser in the back and about 20 minutes into my act he started yelling, 'I love you Rusty' and 'Yeah, you're the best Rusty' and all this stuff—just continually. He was a fan and it was nice, but he was throwing off my timing when I was trying to build or tell a joke. Some folks started shushing him. So finally Eva, my road manager, who was in the front row, said in a stage whisper, 'Will somebody put something in that guy's mouth to quiet him down so we can do the show?' Well, the whole place howled. Eva was this little thing and you just didn't expect something like that out of her. I said, 'Why didn't I think of that?' It was a great show. So much fun.

"Afterwards we set up a table for autographs and to sell LPs. It was a great crowd. The guy who kept yelling came up to the table and he was so sweet, saying he didn't mean to be obnoxious." (*Leatherman*, 2011).

"I saw three shows at Man's Country," said Marge Summit. "Sally Rand, Wayland Flowers, and Rusty Warren. All three were terrific. I got shit for going there. Some women came at me saying that was a boy's place and how could I go there. I didn't care. I never created a problem, so I never had a problem, that simple. Besides, I was a big fan of whoever was booking the talent because they were doing a terrific job."

Playwright and drag legend Charles Busch explained a little about his gig playing Man's Country. "I was living in New York and put a press kit together and sent it out to different places. Man's Country answered. I was thrilled to play there. I was a member when I was at Northwestern. For my act I did these character pieces and called it, *Charles Busch: Alone with a Cast of Thousands.* No costumes, no drag, just me. Unfortunately, spoken character performance didn't really hold anyone's attention. In the audience there were lots of people lying around on pillows who really just wanted to fuck."

"I played Man's Country when I was fairly new to the business," said singer Pamala Stanley. "I knew I was going to a club, but I didn't know it was a bathhouse. I had never played at a bathhouse before. I got all dressed up and went out on stage and everyone was sitting there in towels. It was shock, but the energy was good and the room was so much fun. You just go with it. We had a great show!"

"I saw Carol Jiani there," said Joey McDonald, recalling the singer's 1981 appearance. "She came at exactly the right time. Her song, 'Hit N' Run Lover,' was new and getting a lot of play. She was so fun. Jiani invited people on the dance floor with her. She was there singing and dancing and we were are all dancing beside her and around her in our towels and with our ethyl rags."

"It was fun!" recalled the late comic Judy Tenuta (1949-2022). "I felt like the Bette Midler of Chicago. I will never forget one of the most memorable events. I was asked to perform for Halloween of 1985, and my parents insisted on coming with me. I said. 'Mom & Dad, I don't think you're ready for this jelly!' They are soooooooooo Catholic but at the same time kind of hip. After all, I am their daughter. Anyway, I'm performing and my parents are off to the side as the hot boys in towels are rolling all over, and afterward, my Mom says, 'Oh honey that was so sweet the way your jokes made them want to hug and kiss on the floor...there should be more love like that in the world.' So like me, my Mom was always rooting for the Gays." (*Leatherman* 2011).

"I remember Judy Tenuta," said Jimmy D'Ambrosia. "I went to the show with my ex, who was also my best friend. He had just shaved his head the day before and Judy Tenuta came out with her accordion and looked at him and said, 'Oh my God, important crowd tonight, Gandhi is in the house.'"

In 1984, comic Julie Brown ("I Like 'Em Big and Stupid") debuted the video of her new song, 'The Homecoming Queen's Got a Gun,' on the screen at Man's Country as well as performed. The song and video have since become a cult sensation. The same year songstress Viola Wills (1939-2009) debuted a new music video during a high-energy performance at the bathhouse. Wills was a dynamic vocalist, mostly known for her dance version of "If You Could Read My Mind" as well as the single "Gonna Get Along Without Ya Now."

Richard Knight, Jr. played Man's Country with his band, Knightklub, in 1985. "We were booked for a forty-five-minute set for four hundred and fifty dollars, a fortune," said Knight. "The other guys in the band were straight, but completely open-minded. The room was packed with guys in towels who were enthusiastic about our show." Later that year, Knightklub returned to Man's Country and made three music videos. Added Knight, "...But by that fall I had musically moved in another direction and never finished them."

High-NRG singer and songwriter Holly Oas, who had hits with "He's a Rebel" and a dance version of "Our Day Will Come," also came to Man's Country in the 1980s.

Chicago actress and cabaret legend, Honey West, performed at Man's Country after being approached by Ron Ehemann. "I basically did karaoke, singing over the tracks on cassettes, which were not easy to find. I did mostly standards. I did 'That's All' by Bobby Darren, and 'Money (That's What I Want)' by the Flying Lizards, and probably 'Over the Rainbow'—maybe a couple other things. The crowd was in towels and some were naked. They were appreciative and seemed to enjoy the show."

Dance showcases and theater previews were another part of the legacy of the Man's Country Music Hall. "I went to a one-time only production of Dylan Thomas' *Under Milk Wood* at Man's Country," said MS. "I remember it was performed with music. There was piano accompaniment and a decent sized cast. We were all in our towels in the audience, but as far as I know nothing happened during the show."

Derek Spenser recalled another evening. "The first time I saw a show there, I can't even remember who it was. That wasn't the big thing for me. It was so strange just being there and seeing a show. Whoever I saw was a comic because I recall the audience laughing. I was looking at these smiling faces and I calmed down. There was a sense of community here. People didn't necessarily know each other or interact with each other, but they were all laughing together. I was still closeted, and I can't tell you how huge it was to see that many gay men together, and all laughing, all having a good time."

Chapter Four

Chuck Renslow always insisted that the appeal of Man's Country was more than purely sexual. "It's to be with your own kind. For men who are interested in a mellow evening, the bathhouse has entertainment, a sauna, whirlpool, and a juice bar."

"Man's Country was a place to let your freak flag fly," proclaimed Joey McDonald. "Some people were there not only to play, but to dance all night."

"It was Mecca for anything a gay guy could want," added Chris W.

"The first time I went to Man's Country was in 1974," said Race Bannon. "I came through the door and the first guy I saw was limping. There was grease on his foot. I asked him what was wrong, and he said, 'Oh, someone just sat on my foot. That was my introduction to Man's Country."

Bannon continued, "My late lover, Kevin Lockwood, was Mr. Man's Country of 1974. He was good-looking, but also extremely talented. For the talent part of the contest, he did a slide show of his sculpture and fashions and design. He designed all the clothes he wore that night and then in the question-and-answer portion, before Wanda Lust could ask the question, he ran off stage and came back with a three-foot doll of Wanda Lust that he had made. When the audience saw the replica, they went wild. When he won Mr. Man's Country, he also won a free membership for life."

Pat Batt began coming to Man's Country in the 1970s when he drove down from Milwaukee. "My membership card, which I still have, is four digits. I was a member there even before my case." In late 1977, Batt made Wisconsin headlines after being fired from his job as manager of a nursing Home in Milwaukee for being gay. "They found out I was gay and they wanted me to quit. When I refused, they fired me," explained

Batt. Benefits were held in Milwaukee to fund Batt's lawsuit. When Chuck became aware of the case, he had a fundraiser for Batt at Man's Country. The event, which was hosted by Wanda Lust, helped raise money for Batt and bring awareness to the case and to the larger issue of employer discrimination against LGBT people.

Eventually, Chuck even hired Batt to manage the Gold Coast. "He also hired my boyfriend at the time, Paul, to work at Man's Country." Saturday evenings, Batt frequently came to Man's Country after closing the Gold Coast. "I'd be amped up from work. I went there (Man's Country) to decompress. It became a Saturday ritual. Man's Country had a live DJ until eight in the morning. Then they started playing this canned music that was meant to get everyone up and moving. That was usually about when I left. I went there because my boyfriend worked there, and I knew they played good music. For me it was more a social center. I went there to relax and to interact with people more than for sex."

However, Batt added that wasn't always the case. "When I went to Man's Country, I didn't get a towel. I used to walk around in Levi's without a shirt. The hottest time I had there was once I was walking around and saw this guy in the doorway of his room. I was standing in the hall, and he was a few feet away. We were attracted to one another at a distance and we both just stood there and jacked off staring at each other."

"My roommate Ed and I were too gay for the gay student group at Northwestern," laughed performer Charles Busch. "By senior year we discovered Man's Country. The first time I went was in 1976. It was exhausting—all the walking, those hallways and those aisles. I remember the disco soundtrack—"Love to Love You Baby" and "Love's Theme." I wasn't terribly picky about whose room I went into. I didn't have a type. I was curious about all parts of the man spectrum. At Man's Country I was a little like Dorothy and the world had turned to Technicolor."

For Busch, Man's Country also provided a form of therapy. "I grew up fearing male places like locker rooms or sports teams, even watching sports. I got none of that male bonding stuff. Those things felt threatening to me. But at Man's Country, you could be involved in say a circle-jerk and when each guy cums everyone cheers and there's this rush, this real communal male feeling, that testosterone camaraderie. I found a kind of non-threatening aggressive male joy there that I had never experienced before."

Richard F. was a member at the same time. "My friends and I got fake ID's. We came into the city we went to the gay bars like Broadway Sam's and the original Bistro. I always looked older than I was. Eventually, I used my fake ID to get in Man's Country. I crashed at Man's Country, so I didn't drive back to the suburbs drunk. So it became my go to place after the bars. There was sex, entertainment, and food there. Since it was the 1970s, there was lots of positive sex energy. At the time it was almost a political thing to celebrate your sexuality. I always went there alone. Some guys went with their friends, not me. The thing was, even though I was alone I felt connected to a broader community at Man's County. For me, it was a way to merge community and sex in a positive way."

"I had heard of the place," said Dean Ogren. "I heard it was three floors with sex everywhere. Well, that sounded like someplace I want to go. The first time I went I was so nervous. I was very unsure of myself, very thin. I didn't feel attractive, but people were friendly and interested. I was worn out within an hour. This beat the hell out of the dirty bookstores on Wells Street. There was more activity here and it was a more relaxed atmosphere. Man's Country was a good place for the classic cruise. No need to talk. It was all about that sexual dance. You never knew who you would see there. If you left Man's Country and you didn't have a good time—it was your own damn fault."

Ogren added, "One room on the main floor was two levels, like a duplex. On the bottom level was a scene set up with a sling. Then, up some stairs was a loft platform with a mattress on it. Sometimes I hung out outside that room because I knew whoever had that room was probably into leather or kink. That was another thing. Man's Country was a place to explore, maybe try something you haven't tried."

Another advantage of frequenting the baths was their relative safety from harassment or arrest. There had not been a raid on a Chicago bathhouse in years, yet entrapment was still happening during this era and into the 1980s. Gay men were still hooking up and getting busted in parks and public restrooms. As a private club, the risk of something like that happening at Man's Country was slim to none.

Mostly life at the bathhouse was an ongoing party, the celebration of the freedoms that came with Gay Liberation kept the good times coming. On New Year's Eve 1977, Wanda asked Mr. Man's Country to be in the holiday variety show. He agreed. "Wanda wanted to turn him into a human disco ball," recalled Chichester. "We glued pieces of mirror all over him and said, 'We want you get on this giant turntable and spin around until we tell you to get off, and we did—eventually. But the turntable just kept going around and around. He was spinning a long time."

"I have my membership card somewhere," said Dave Plomin, who first went to Man's Country in the late 1970s. "I met a guy at [the bar] Broadway Limited who sponsored me to be a member. We went there and after we did it, he gave me the grand tour. Then he told me to check out the place on my own. It was a maze of rooms. Exploring it was like an exercise course with walking around and going up and down the stairs. I ended up returning to Man's Country quite a few times. I liked the secretiveness of going in. The outside of the building was pretty low-key—no flashy sign. Most people had no idea what went on inside. At Man's Country you might see anyone. And it was a place for everyone— all types of bodies, older men too. It was like a 1970s gay porn movie— everybody was having sex with everybody."

Man's Country was where anything might happen—and often did. It was the sort of place where the items in the lost and found included a glass eye and an uncooked chicken that had been discovered on the steam room floor.

One evening, a member approached the front desk complaining about a gash in his skin and a missing patch of public hair. Shortly after, another member has the same complaint. Chichester investigated. He noticed a small clump of pubes on the carpet in the hall. In a few more feet, he discovered another clump. When Chichester eventually tracked down the culprit, he had a handful of pubes in the pocket his wraparound towel. Chichester added, "We took this young guy to his locker and inside were Baggies of public hair. He had been going in the orgy and blowjob areas and used cuticle scissors to cut patches of pubes. He was banned after that."

Chichester said the strange events were few and far between and the tough parts of the job were more than balanced by the benefits. Chichester shared his favorite part of his tenure as the manager of Man's Country. "There was the thrill of watching people come in and lose their inhibitions, along with their towels. You could see them becoming free. That was the best part of the job. We had entertainment, a place to eat, even a shop. I considered it almost more of a men's club than a bathhouse."

Man's Country was an escape from the everyday world. Some members even arrived at Man's Country with luggage, prepared to stay for the weekend. In addition to personal "sex stuff"—members brought things to enhance the décor—beads to hang from the doorframe, throw rugs, colored lights, incense, and anything else to make the room their own for the duration.

"Sometimes I checked in for the weekend," said Race Bannon. "They let you do that at the time. There was a snack shop, a sex store, a theater, dancing, sex—there was everything I needed right there. So much of that time was about more than fucking. I loved the casualness of the sex, like you could be there talking with a friend in the snack shop and then just say, 'Okay, I'm going to go have sex now.' I loved the way the sexual mixed with the social. That didn't exist in any other environment outside of the great bathhouses, and it hasn't been replicated since."

Bannon continued, "Man's Country was a self-contained place, where we could be sequestered from the rest of the world that didn't get us. It was not just hot and sexy—there was a sense of camaraderie and safety to just hang out and to be gay in this all gay-male world. That was so important at the time. I remember having political conversations there and talks at Man's Country about the gay liberation movement. I heard the first talk there about planning a protest about Anita Bryant's appearance in Chicago. The bathhouse was connected and at the same time completely apart. This place was not all sex club banter."

"Weekends my friends would go to Man's Country," recalled Joey McDonald. "We would get a row of rooms and sometimes stay Friday through Sunday. We did different substances, experimented. We weren't driving. We had a bed and food. For us it was more the socializing, like a slumber party, and more like a clubhouse than a bathhouse. The sex was there, but there was a lot more. Other groups of friends went there too. Sometimes my friends and I went in costume. Other guys came in costume too. There was a group who came in with tambourines and ran through the halls and danced with the tambourines in the Music Hall. Crazy stuff. That was how the bathhouse scene was then."

At the time, McDonald also worked at Man's Country. As might be expected, sometimes work got in the way of play. "At the start of my shift the first thing I did was clean the Music Hall. I would turn off the spotlight on the disco ball, bring up the houselights, toss the big lounging pillows in the middle of the dance floor, and vacuum around the sides of the room. We had to vacuum because the little Styrofoam pellets from the throw pillows got everywhere. So this time I started vacuuming and I was having trouble. Chuck came to the front desk earlier, and I guess he asked where I was. They told him I was up in the Music Hall. So Chuck came up and stood quietly and watched me vacuum in this one corner for twenty minutes. I thought something was wrong with the vacuum because I could not pick up the pellets—they kept moving. So, finally Chuck shut off the spotlight on the mirror ball. Once he did all the pellets I was trying to vacuum disappeared. Then he walked up to me and in this very kind tone he said, 'I think you had better take the day off.'"

For many members, Man's Country was an oasis of sexual expression and experimentation—a safe place to push boundaries and explore desire. "I came out in 1969 after years in the closet," said MS. "It's hard to explain how liberating it was to come out and have sex with all kinds of men—to go to the baths, or bars, or even to cruise parks. At the height of its popularity, there were lines down the block to get into Man's Country. Going there made me feel safe. It felt comfortable—like we were all connected or a big family in a way."

"When I first started going there the neighborhood was kind of sketchy," offered Joe B. "The provocative ads in the paper got me there. I needed Man's Country. I grew up overweight and felt awkward. Man's Country did a lot for my self-esteem. I started to see myself differently. I was walking around in a towel and guys were interested. I felt safe here—and free. That was really important. I was closeted during the day. At the time I worked as an accountant. My company would have fired me if they found out. I had to be straight all day, but at Man's Country I could be myself and have fun. There was such power being around people and not having to hide who I was."

Harry Shattuck claimed he all but resided at the bathhouse. "I was Mr. Man's Country in 1975 and then Mr. Windy City in 1976. I was just a little muscle-bound kid fresh out of the navy who loved to dance and take his clothes off. Man's Country was like heaven to someone like me, meaning a nymphomaniac. I was there every night for a couple of years. I got a free year's pass as Mr. Man's Country and then a free lifetime pass as Mr. Windy City and I used it—a lot." (*Leatherman,* 2011).

"Man's Country was my first big bathhouse," added Race Bannon. "Within those confines we could be as gay as we wanted. That was a huge thing. It was not just a place to have sex. It was a community center. Sometimes I would be there for hours and then have sex. That wasn't what brought me there." Bannon also mentioned the on-site leather visibility. "At the time there was as much leather mixed in at Man's Country as I have seen at a bathhouse since. That made an impression. Man's Country was a place to feel comfortable leaning that way, being curious about leather, because some guys there were walking around in their leathers."

"As a young man living in Southwest Michigan, I used to come into Chicago with my friends before I moved here in 1981," said Jeff Berry. "We would come get rooms at Man's Country, which were ten dollars or something—and the amenities were fabulous. Man's Country was a place to explore and for me, it was quite a laboratory."

Israel Wright started coming to Man's Country as a place to go before heading back home. "Early on I would take the train into the city and go to the bars. A lot of times I was there until they closed. Then, I usually went to Man's Country. There was sex, but it was also a place to get it together before I had to get back to the train." Wright explained that for him, "Man's Country was a place to meet people and explore your sexuality and fantasies. I met people at Man's Country that I never saw at the bars. And I felt comfortable there."

"I probably went there for the first time in 1976," recalled Dan Neniskis. "You couldn't just walk in off the street. I had Phil Spence, who bartended at the Gold Coast, write me a letter of recommendation. That got me in. Wow, was all I could think—so many like-minded guys who were into casually fucking without caring and were ready to engage."

"When the place was really hopping," recalled Chichester, "it was like being on stage, only our applause was the sound of a ball sack slapping someone's ass. In those days, there was such a sense of freedom sexually. Guys would be walking around in a daze, having had the time of their life, on their way to have, maybe the next time of their life. The sense of sexual freedom was hard to imagine."

"I went there in the 1970s," recalled a member. "I seldom had sex there. For me it was the visual stimulation as well as the energy and the sound. I was more a voyeur. There was the mystique walking around in there. I was excited by what I might find. I would go up and down the aisles for hours. Sometimes I would go there feeling sad and alone and sometimes I left in the same mood, mainly because the fantasy I had about going there didn't hit home. It was unrealistic. I went there looking for a relationship."

In August of 1976, the sundeck at Man's Country opened. Access was up a spiral staircase outside the Music Hall, through a door, and into the sunlight or the moonlight. The sundeck had some plants and a fountain. The mats were great for sunning and sex.

"It was like a refuge up there," recalled Israel Wright. "The roof was quieter with less activity than on the floors below. I remember it as more a place to go to take a break from things."

"I remember the spiral staircase to get up there," added Dan Neniskis, "and then a landing with three walls and an outside door that accessed the roof. The deck wasn't very large—some benches in a formation and raised flowerbeds as well. At night it was pretty active—not as active as downstairs, but active. It was one of those places where people went to watch or to be watched."

On weekends at Man's Country, a continental breakfast was served on the sundeck. "As evening wore on," explained Chichester, "the music went from dance to more sensuous and then it became quieter. At eight in the morning, Wanda [Lust] would start do a light show and slowly raise the volume of the music to get everyone up and awake before announcing there were pastries, juice, and coffee on the sundeck."

"Man's Country was a great place to go after the bars closed and you weren't ready to go home," said Ron Ehemann. "It was someplace to take the party at four in the morning. It was a place to crash as well. Sunday afternoons was classical music with big pillows around the dance floor and people would be lying around having sex or just crashed out."

"I liked going to the Music Hall and lying on those pillows around the sides," explained MS. "It was mellower up there. There was some cruising, some couples having a moment, and some were just lying there listening to the music. Wanda Lust was an excellent DJ, but they all were at Man's Country."

"I liked the vibe," recalled Richard F. "with the pillows everywhere. I used to crash out and soak in the atmosphere. People were having sex around and there was music. There was the smell of sex and poppers and chlorine and the feel of the carpet and those big pillows—all that added to the atmosphere. I remember that place in a very sensual way—not just in an erotic way. I remember it with all my senses."

"I grew up at Paulina and Ainslie and worked across the street at the paint store. When I first started going to Man's Country," explained Spike aka Michael King. "I went there to get away and to be peaceful. I could go there. I was a member and I would be safe. Eventually, I met my first partner when he was working the front desk."

"Man's Country was an after-hours place for bar people," explained TL Noble. "You ran into everyone there. I would go there with Kim Spaulding after the Bistro or Paradise closed. The place was always interesting. I remember the decorated rooms—one with black lights and another draped with these bohemian scarves everywhere. I loved the whirlpool and grotto area," added Noble. "It was so strange. Once when it wasn't too busy, I got in the hot tub and put in a bunch of bubbles, so it was like a big bubble bath from a Doris Day movie. They had to drain the pool and everything."

"I liked to go pick up a guy in the wet area," said Joe B, "and then we would go up and fool around on those big pillows around the dance floor. I never got a room."

"My favorite was the steam room," recalled another member. "I loved the feel of the heat on my body, and it was so dark in there you could hardly see. I liked the mystery of moving deeper into the steam."

Israel Wright also recalled the steam room. "I remember going in there and thinking about where to position myself so I was close to the activity. The showers outside the steam room were spigots on a column that are made for checking each other out. And the hot tub was right there."

Dan Neniskis was another fan of the wet area. "I liked the grotto and the opaque green of the hot tub with the white light beneath the surface. The chlorine smell in that area was strong. There were hooks outside the steam room to hang your towel. There was always a lot going on in there. Sometimes I went to Man's Country when I felt a cold coming on to sweat it out in the steam room. Of course, I played while I was in there, but the steam worked."

Neniskis also recalled the locker room. "I loved the feeling of getting out of my clothes and the anticipation of the great time I was going to have. It was fresh for me that way for quite a while. Then, it changed for me. Instead of a destination, going to Man's Country came more as an afterthought. I still had a great time, but it was where I went if I didn't get laid someplace else."

"I went to Man's Country if I didn't get lucky at the bars," said Rick Karlin. "It was that simple. But once I got there, I could always get laid, so sometimes I ended up socializing too."

"Sometimes after work a bunch of us from the Bistro would share a cab there," recalled Scott Taylor. "Usually someone got a big room and we would all congregate there—but it was about sex so we would wander off and get some and then regroup. It was so fun. You could see almost anything. Sometimes the party lasted the night—especially if we didn't work the next day. Those big pillows in the Music Hall were wonderful. Once I was in there, having sex off the dance floor and Donna Summer's *Love to Love You Baby* was playing, and I almost started to laugh because it was ridiculous to be having sex to that song."

"We were a destination," recalled Chichester. "Sometimes Rod Scheel who owned the big gay complex in Madison, would rent a bus and come to Man's Country and all those Wisconsin boys would file out. Man's Country was a big gay field trip." (Scheel died of AIDS at age 39 in 1990).

The first time Derek Spenser went to Man's Country, he went with a friend who had been there before. "I was so nervous, and then I had to give them my ID. Once I was inside, I had fun. The place was packed. I explored. It was a labyrinth. I didn't know what anything meant. I didn't know what an open door meant or what it meant if a guy was sitting up or lying face down. I ended up in the orgy room. It was pitch black. Next thing I knew I felt hands. I just gave myself over to pleasure. It felt so freeing."

Spenser continued, "I went back a few times a year for a while. I got comfortable with my nakedness there. I found self-assurance. I felt part of things there. At Man's Country I forgot about the outside world—about stress and issues. Time suspended there. What I learned about myself [there] played a big part in being the person I am today. I learned about gay culture there, bathhouse etiquette, and language, and I even learned about clothes. I actually looked at what guys were wearing in the locker room before they undressed. I learned all that by going there."

"I was from a small town and didn't know places like this existed," said Jim Meischmer. "At first, I was scared, but then I was there every Friday and Saturday. I liked hanging out on the pillows in the Music Hall and socializing. I liked to walk around. I was a complete voyeur. Let's see who's in the sling tonight. Always exciting. I liked the feeling of community, and of being a regular. I went in drag once. They knew me so they let me in, but then I ended up falling down the stairs on the way to the snack bar. For New Year's I decorated my room and had champagne and everything."

"My first time was in 1983," said NW. "I was in college and struggling with my sexuality. A friend took me to the gay bars in Chicago. At the end of the evening, we went to Man's Country. I had no idea what it was. I had no idea those places existed. That first time was late on a Saturday. They buzzed us through the door. The place was packed. I couldn't believe it. Hot gay men were sucking and fucking and doing everything else in the rooms in the hallways, downstairs, upstairs on those big pillows in the Music Hall. I thought I had died and gone to heaven. It was glorious—a gay adult playground that was sexy, dirty, proud, joyous, and wonderful. You could even dance there. The music was good. The sound was good. Any time I had the opportunity in the next couple years, I went back. Man's Country was exhilarating, pure fun, and removed from the real world."

"I liked that I could walk around freely," said Jimmy D'Ambrosia. "I was self-conscious about my body. Man's Country helped with that. I liked walking around and feeling hot. I started walking around in a jockstrap. I liked the feel of walking around in a jock and a cut-off jersey. It wasn't really me, but I looked good. I liked dressing that way and I usually got lucky."

Queer thinker and writer Jon-Henri Damski wrote of Man's Country in a 1985 *Windy City Times* column. "A first timer once told me he couldn't believe where he was. Every time he went in and out of a room, he thought he should have to pay more money. He thought it was a whorehouse. With hundreds of guys passing through on a weekend, outsiders might think Man's Country was just a stranger's paradise, full of anonymous sex and multiple partners. Not so. The whole crowd broke into sub-groups of regulars. There was the snack bar crowd, the dancers and the fan dancers, the pillow huggers, the leather clubs, the cowboys, the loud-talking queens, and the silent ones who never said anything.

The column continued. "In their groups everyone seemed to know each other. Maybe you wouldn't know everyone's last name, but you pretty well knew what they did on the outside and kept in touch. But if some government authority or public health official called you and wanted their names, you would not give it to them... At Man's Country, we knew each other like brothers of a clan. We trusted each other in sex and morals, and didn't trust that our society would treat us morally."

In a column several years before, Damski had explored a bit further his take on bathhouse allure. "Baths, for me, were a communal, not an individual, experience. I was not there alone for ego gratification, or genital release. Rooms were only partitions of the mind. It didn't matter if I stayed in mine and beat off, or if I joined the herd in the orgy room. The total feeling was communal. I shared the gay male experience in all its colors, sounds, tastes, and smells. I experienced—first and second hand—my mind of love: male homosexuality in all its forms and poses."

Award-winning author Edmund White used his formidable literary prowess to chronicle to talk about a visit to Man's Country in his 1980 gay sex travelogue, *States of Desire*. "One night I went to Man's Country, Chicago's most popular baths. On the ground floor are the showers, a steam room, and a hot tub, all fitted into a stone grotto. On the second floor are rooms, lockers, the TV room, and the orgy room—TV viewing and orgy viewing seemed tranquil. Upstairs I found the disco. Lying on mats along the wall were sleeping bodies. A twirling mirror ball cast scintillas of light over these dreamers. At one end of the room was a spotlit stage, bracketed by art deco caryatids framing a set: a painted skyline of skinny skyscrapers in black and white, stylized to look hundreds of stories tall. The polished dance floor was empty until a black man in red-striped, calf length athletic socks, a jock strap, a red t-shirt, and a baseball cap began to dance by himself. He was joined by an outrageous white fatty, who performed 'interpretative'—of what, I couldn't be sure. Coiled metal stairs led me up to a roof garden, where, under a cool, blowy sky, I watched two couples fucking."

Man's Country exterior. Photo: courtesy Ron Ehemann.

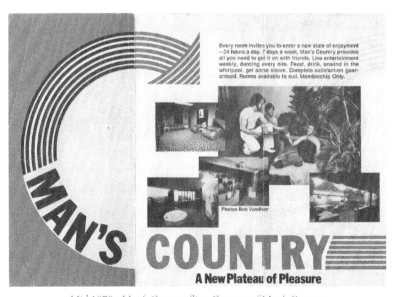

Mid 1970s. Man's Country flier. Courtesy of Man's Country.

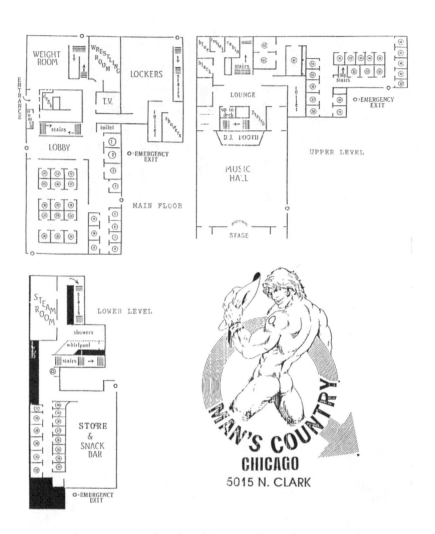

Early Man's Country floor plan. Courtesy: Leather Archives & Museum.

Mid 1970s flier photo.

Vintage Man's Country Ad with image by Etienne.

Sally Rand photo. Courtesy of Ron Ehemann.

Sally Rand, Wanda Lust, and the staff celebrate Gary Chichester's birthday. Photo: Gary Chichester.

Man's Country New York double-billboard above Village Cigars, 1977.
Photo: @JackFalat.com

Wanda Lust/Nurse Lust outside the Mobile STD Testing Unit
(aka the VD Van). Photo courtesy of Ron Ehemann.

Chuck Renslow wishing the final three contestants of Mr. Man's Country good luck. Photo: Ron. Ehemann.

Tom of Finland, Chuck, and Dom. Photo A.J. Epstein from Chuck Renslow Collection at Leather Archives & Museum.

Chapter Five

Given Chuck's love of photography and the male form, combined with Dom's artwork as well as his appreciation for gay art in general, Man's Country became a gallery of photos and drawings celebrating the erotic and the beauty of the male form. As with the Gold Coast, Dom's artwork as Etienne enhanced an already sexually charged atmosphere.

At Man's Country, Dom did several large murals, including the enormous paintings on plywood lining either side of the grand staircase. This multi-paneled mural showed a parade of male flesh and half-clad fantasy men climbing the stairs as well. At the top was another Etienne mural, a beefy muscled muse strumming a lyre with the words Music Hall on an unfurled scroll above him.

Another Etienne mural was at the head of the stairs leading to the lower level. The mural was of a redheaded muscle stud holding a towel. His eyes looked to the left, showing interest. His pose was one of availability and promise. The tattoo on his bicep was the male symbol, which was also the logo for Man's Country. "I liked that mural because it was so large, so dramatic and sexy," said one patron. "It seemed to be what Man's Country was all about. It was so male and so dominant."

Etienne also painted a mural behind the downstairs snack bar and a rectangular oil painting, *Car Wash*, which was above one of the doorways in the locker room—*Car Wash* currently resides in the Etienne Auditorium at the Leather Archives and Museum in Chicago.

Dom and his iconic art as Etienne were the subject of a 1977 profile by Bill Lumen in *Gay Life* newspaper, 'Real Life Artist Draws Fantasies.' In the piece, Dom explains how drawing and painting came naturally to him and that there was never any question what he wanted to draw. "My contemporaries in high school had their paper routes while I drew naked sailors."

In the piece, Dom also shares that he never really liked the name Etienne. "It's a little flowery. I'd rather have a butch name, like Dirk." When asked about his creative intent, Orejudos responded, "I simply present a sexual fantasy trip through my drawings and hope the viewer understands."

Despite a lack of formal art training, aside from a couple frustrating months at the Art Institute, Dom created images that resonated with gay men worldwide. He had a knack for capturing, with great clarity, the heat of his vivid erotic imagination. In the piece, Dom also shared with Lumen that he did not use live models for his oil painting or sketches, responding, "If the model was a hunk, I wouldn't get anything done. My mind would be on other things."

In addition to helping define the atmosphere on the inside of Man's Country, Dom's art also helped define the bathhouse to the outside world. As Etienne, Dom created dozens of Man's Country advertisements just as he had done with the Gold Coast and other Renslow businesses. His art would also be a key factor in the early success of International Mr. Leather. Through the erotically charged images he created for Man's Country advertisements, Dom managed to brand the business, spark the interest of a core audience, and create a good amount of the legendary mystique of the bathhouse.

The walls of Man's Country also featured the work of several masters of male erotic art such as Tom of Finland, Rex, and Bill Ward. Interspersed with these artworks was some of the pioneering male physique photography from Kris Studios. Also on display were signed posters from many of the acts who had performed in the Music Hall— Sally Rand, Wayland Flowers, Charles Pierce, and more.

TL Noble added, "Once when I was there, I said to Chuck, 'There is great art on the walls—but the walls could highlight that and give the crowd even more to look at while they're cruising around here.' So, Chuck let me add some graphics and lines on the walls."

Another piece of art on the premises at Man's Country was a functional phone booth with a folding door on the lower level. When cellphones replaced the need for it, the telephone was removed, but the booth remained in place. The booth was then painted black and then tagged with fluorescent graffiti in the style of artist Keith Haring.

In addition to *Car Wash*, the locker room also had several framed posters on the walls. The locker room was carpeted and featured two double-sided aisles of bi-level brown lockers. The polished wood changing benches on either side of the lockers were cut in a zigzag shape. The long bank of lockers was capped on both ends by a polished piece of fitted wood that read Man's Country.

The shower area and bathroom were three-steps-up from the locker room. The double mirrors were straight ahead. Beside the sinks was a dispenser with black plastic combs that said Man's Country. To the right was a recessed area with a urinal trough and stalls. To the left was a recessed, tiled open shower area with spigots fixed in the tile walls.

"I found Man's Country about 1996," recalled David Weeks. "When I went into that shower area, there were other guys in there. I stood there watching and thinking that at Man's Country the men were finally showering with each other the way I wanted them to shower together."

Exiting the shower and bathroom area and taking a hard left followed by a hard right, members once more walked down a hallway partly comprised of glass blocks lined with gay art. Taking another left before reaching the lobby, a patron would reach the top of the stairs to the lower level.

For years the built-in fish tank at the foot of the lower-level stairs was home to one of the residents of Man's Country. Oscar was an oscar, a carnivorous fish who always became extremely popular around feeding time. Chuck explained Oscar's eventual demise, "The exterminator came in to spray for bugs and he was going around the room and he turned around and his tank he carried on his back smashed the glass of the fish tank and Oscar died on the Man's Country floor." (*Leatherman*, 2011).

To the right of the fish tank was a floor-to-ceiling glass block wall on either side of the condensation-heavy double glass doors. Through the doors were more showers, a steam room, and a whirlpool. In the first few years of business, the Man's Country wet area had been upstairs in the space that eventually became Chuck's office. The reason his office had wooden shingles on the walls was a holdover from that time. Condensation from the hot tub would roll off the wooden shingles rather than warp the walls.

In 1977, the wet area moved to the lower level. When this occurred the new décor reflected the change. The "underground" wet area was reimagined as if it were located beneath the streets of Paris, deep in the city's underbelly. The result was a strange, menacing, and sexy atmosphere. The new whirlpool was the centerpiece and top of the line for a "party tub" of the era.

Once the renovation of the lower level was complete, the reopening of the revamped wet area was covered in a 1977 staff piece in *Gay Life* newspaper: "Man's Country inaugurated it's new 'waterworks area' with the staff throwing a fully clothed Chuck Renslow into the newly completed whirlpool, a christening spray of champagne showering him."

The article continued, "The whirlpool, a masterpiece of rough brick and exposed pipes, is three times the size of the original whirlpool at Man's Country and boasts a rain curtain at the arched entrance of the 'manhole,' a cave-like hideaway at one end of the pool. The rough brick and exposed pipe theme has been carried over into the shower area giving the entire 'waterworks area' a subterranean atmosphere. The heat of the bubbling waters is great therapy for soaking away bodily tensions and the intimacy of the pool affords a place in which to meet new friends."

A clay and brick grotto surrounded the enormous whirlpool. Adjacent to the whirlpool was a shower area of several water spigot poles, exposed red brick, and clay tiling. One wall of the shower alcove had hooks for towels.

A few feet away, another row of towel hooks was outside "the largest steam room in the Midwest." The interior of the steam room was dark, which combined with the steam, often made the visibility inside close to nonexistent. There were two benches in the room and built-in tile seating ran along three of the walls. The fourth wall was comprised of glass blocks. The only constant light in the steam room came through that glass brick wall. For some members, the lack of visibility was a significant part of the allure. One member described it as "walking blind into a room of hands."

Another unique and popular feature at Man's Country was a gay men's store called Erogenous Zone—A Shop of Things That Feel Good. Erogenous Zone was around the corner at the top of the main stairs outside the Music Hall. The shop had an actual storefront, complete with display windows. Though the space itself was extremely compact at approximately 150 square feet, every inch of the space was bursting with inventory. Erogenous Zone stocked mostly "tub" related items and gay fashions—caftans, jocks, tube socks, and tie pants. Also lining the shelves of the retail space were aromas, poppers, magazines, lube, cock rings, cards, handcuffs, sex toys, and more.

Patrick Jordan ran the store and was listed on the business license. Jordan was also Gary Chichester's lover at the time. "We sold clothing for dancing—like short shorts, jockstraps, and cut offs," recalled Chichester. "Gauze wraparound harem pants were very popular too. Poppers were the bestselling item at the store, but we also sold a lot of lube."

After five years, Erogenous Zone closed, and the space was revamped as the Country Store, open seven days a week. The contents of the store did not dramatically change. The Country Store had much of the same tubs merchandise as Erogenous Zone, as well as hankies, key chains, jerseys, and "the latest in latex goods."

Member Joey McDonald recalled the Country Store for another reason, "Jimmy Stiveir worked there. He had a big San Francisco moustache and he would be standing there in a cowboy hat, boots, and a jockstrap. He was so hot. I would just stand there and stare at him."

In a 1985 piece, Chicago queer Jon-Henri Damski wrote. "Hundreds of guys used to hang out, pass through, and live at Man's Country on weekends. They would come from Michigan and Indiana, Montrose and Cal City, New York, Paris, Houston. And Toronto. Noted figures from theater, dance, arts, sports, business, and politics often stayed overnight and enjoyed the privileges at the club."

Damski continued, "They [Man's Country] had a steam room and a whirlpool, a TV room, fantasy rooms, and play areas where you could cruise like inside an indoor park. They don't force you to wear towels only. You can come in leather or Levis, or male uniform drag, and cruise your heart out. Man's Country was the most visually exciting male bazaar in the Midwest."

As Damski mentioned, Man's Country was a travel destination. In the early days of gay liberation, gay travel became increasingly popular—a new consumer trend. In increasing numbers, gay men were visiting gay areas in other cities and experiencing gay life there. For many gay people, community loyalty began to increasingly extend beyond local businesses.

"Gaycations" were defined by pleasure, fun, and celebrating the newly won gay freedoms. Gay travel guides like *the Spartacus Guide* (began in 1970), *The Gayellow Pages* (1974) and the *Bob Damron Address Book* (started secretly in 1965) surged in popularity with the growing gay travel phenomenon.

The gay travel magazine *Ciao!* (1973-1980), began publication during this period. In each issue the magazine covered gay destinations from Helsinki to Des Moines. The magazine included gay travel tips as well as a centerfold dude. *Ciao!* had reviews of the gay bars, restaurants, baths, hotels, and cruising spots of 8-10 cities in every issue.

An additional component to the popularity of gay travel remained the closet. Big cities provided anonymity. Sometimes these closet-opening vacations meant a pure immersion into sex, and sometimes the appeal was to simply be among other gay people. Either way, the gay men who visited Chicago often ended up at Man's Country.

Chapter Six

In 1975, an epidemiologist arrived at Man's Country. "He was an asshole," said Gary Chichester. "He threatened to close us down. I ended up telling him to leave. Two weeks later, a couple guys arrived and said I had been reported as a syphilis contact—which I believe was that first guy. Anyway, they had to take my blood. The thing was, these other two guys who showed up to do that [Bill and Tony] were nice. They were a part of a new and more understanding generation of physicians. They were actually concerned about sexually transmitted diseases in the gay community."

Out of this relationship came the start of STD testing at Man's Country. The weekly on-site testing program began and soon flourished. Testing became so popular the Chicago Gay Health Project opened a small clinic upstairs.

In 1975, Chicago's *Gay Life* covered the opening of the Man's Country on-site clinic. "In an effort to help control the spread of venereal disease, Man's Country/Chicago (a membership club) has begun an independent testing clinic between 10PM–2AM every Saturday night. With the help of two health officials, Bill and Tony, and a handful of dedicated volunteers from Chicago's gay community, Man's Country is making an effort to help stamp out VD."

The *Gay Life* piece continued, "In the strictest of confidence, Bill and Tony take blood for syphilis, and anal, oral, and frontal cultures for detection of gonorrhea. They also answer any questions that may arise."

Being solely a free testing clinic, Bill and Tony could not provide treatment on site. Instead, they informed the men who tested positive for STDs/STIs. They also offered to make the results available for treatment by city health clinics or personal physicians.

With easy sex as part of the new gay urban reality, accessible and non-judgmental STI/STD testing, followed by proper treatment, was the solution. Maintaining proper sexual health was the responsible thing for sexually active people to do. STD/STI testing could even be a part of the party.

Around this time, manager Gary Chichester was hospitalized with hepatitis. In an effort to lift his spirits, Wanda Lust dressed as a nurse and went with a friend to visit Gary in the hospital—bringing a joint along for fun. That evening an important chapter in Chicago gay men's sexual health was born—Nurse Lust.

Once the clinic opened at the bathhouse, Wanda became the poster diva for STD testing. She appeared on posters promoting the VD testing program in a pose reminiscent of the Uncle Sam poster, only Nurse Lust was saying, "I Want You, to Get Tested." On the nights the clinic was open, Wanda transformed into Nurse Lust, swapping her evening gowns for a white uniform and (sometimes) sensible shoes. Wanda made the clinic fun and turned STD/STI testing into a party.

In September 1975, Nurse Lust accompanied the STD mobile testing unit, also known as the VD van, as it made its rounds, parking outside various gay nightspots. When the VD van pulled up, Nurse Lust would leap from the vehicle and run into the nearby gay bars to get patrons to come to the van and get tested. And if you went with Nurse Lust to get poked or swabbed, she gave you a cookie. The success was immediate and astounding. In the first week the VD van rolled onto the streets over 1,000 people were tested.

Karen Ross recalled, "I'd be there tending bar at Sunday's, and the VD van would pull up. You've got to picture this—a big VD van parked outside gay bars between ten and midnight, trying to get people tested. And running around in the middle of all this, a really tall drag queen dressed as a nurse. Need I say more?" (*Leatherman*, 2011).

"There was a great deal of support from the bars," said Chichester. "I called bars and said, 'Hey, we want to come have the VD van park by your place so your customers can get checked for VD.' All the bars were happy to help."

The week after being tested by the VD van, the numbers—not names—of those with positive test results were published *in Gay Life* newspaper. VD Results Out became a regular feature. The following is an example of the copy that accompanied the positive numbers. "Results are now available from the test for syphilis given late in September on the VD Bus. If your number appears on the list shown, then you should see your personal physician, or a gay VD clinic as soon as possible. Inform your physician or the clinic that your test results on the VD Bus were positive."

At the bottom of the shaded box was the copy, "If your number is listed above, the following gay clinics are available to treat you: Howard Brown Memorial Clinic, 1250 W. Belden, every Wednesday from 7PM–10PM. The new gay VD clinic is operated by the Chicago Board of Health."

Chicago's other gay news source in 1975, *The Chicago Gay Crusader,* also praised the mobile STD testing unit. "Personnel aboard the travelling VD bus took blood samples from 1,007 clients during its Sept 23-29 tour of Chicago's gay community, despite Board of Health expectations that no more than 500 would visit it."

The article continued, "Wanda Lust, the Man's Country entertainer who toured with the bus, recalled how "uptight" some potential patrons were. "At Le Pub, we had to tell them we were using Gucci needles," she cracked. But general manager Gary Chichester praised three Board of Health technicians on the bus—Bill, Tony, and Rob—for their skills and ability to put clients at ease."

Three years later, in 1978, *Gay Life* newspaper covered the program's continued success. "The Chicago Gay Health Project has announced that the VD Van this year treated 751 people, an increase of 40 over last year. This time the volunteers on the van were doing gonorrhea testing as well as testing for syphilis."

"The Chicago Gay Health Project is a coalition made up of the Howard Brown Memorial Clinic, the Chicago Department of Health Venereal Disease Control Program, and individuals concerned with public health and work with the gay community. Besides the VD Van, the project does both screening and location screening. This past year the project also developed a brochure on sexually transmitted diseases for gay men and women for the City of Chicago Department of Health. That brochure is now being used in the city's clinics."

In the summer of 1978, a patron with crutches checked into Man's Country. Unfortunately, during the evening, he somehow fell into the whirlpool and drowned. Police arrived on the scene. The body was removed, and the police tape was put in place. The Health Department was also coming.

Apparently, Wanda felt for the patron, but as the hostess of Man's Country she also regretted how the accident had soured everyone's evening. Eager to elevate the mood, Wanda went upstairs and got a mannequin she had in the DJ booth, brought it downstairs, and tossed it in the whirlpool. A moment later, Chuck ushered the people from the Health Department into the area. He was not happy, and Wanda found herself on his shit list.

Wanda had been considering a move. More than once she had told people that Wanda Lust was her name as well as her nature. She thought that now might be the time. Her relocation to Kansas City was fairly seamless. Wanda began working at the Club Baths in Kansas City doing much of what she had done at Man's Country—stage manager, resident emcee, DJ, and hostess. However, without a proper stage, Wanda performed around the perimeter of a swimming pool.

In Kansas City, Wanda also continued her work on behalf of gay men's health, recreating the mobile STD testing unit. In Kansas City, the mobile testing unit was not a van but a M*A*S*H* unit jeep. Wanda was soon the toast of Kansas City. Within months, a club in Houston made her an offer. In February 1980, Wanda was planning to relocate when she was murdered, stabbed after a showing of the film *The Fog* by a man she had shushed during the movie. Wanda Lust died on the sidewalk, cradled in her lover's arms with the wail of an ambulance still blocks away.

As Nurse Lust, Wanda brought her own brand of bawdy positivity to the experience of getting tested. She gave people a cookie and a couple of laughs to replace the shameful nature of what STD testing had been less than a decade before.

Chapter Seven

As the product of gay liberation, Man's Country had a vested interest in national politics, especially those pertaining to LGBTQ rights and issues. Man's Country was even more involved locally, giving back to the Chicago community with a consistent record of support and involvement to various gay and lesbian groups and causes.

The 1976 Man's Country pinup calendar was sold at the front desk, at the Erogenous Zone, and select spots around town. The three-dollar donation was asked for the calendar. The money collected for the calendars went to benefit the Pride Week Planning Committee. The group planned and coordinated all the festivities around Pride including the parade.

The same year, the Pride Committee was also the beneficiary of the Man's Country sock hop. The dance was open to both men and women and featured entertainment by the Wanda Lust Pride Revue and Franne Golde. *Gay Life* newspaper covered the event. "Put on your dancing shoes and waltz over to Man's Country for their '76 Gay Pride Week Benefit. It's a dance marathon starting at 10pm May 29th and ending at 10 pm on May 31st. The purpose of the marathon is to raise funds for the Gay Pride Planning Committee and of course to have a good time."

Another Man's Country fundraiser was the bathhouse version of a High School Homecoming. That weekend, the Man's Country Trojans paired off against a team from a local bar or the Tavern Guild in a football game at the Chicago outdoor queerspace, the Belmont Rocks. After the big football game there was a homecoming dance at Man's Country. The Homecoming dance was where Mr. Football Hero was crowned. The title was not a popularity contest but was another fundraising opportunity. The winner was the individual who collected the most money for the Tavern Guild's Frank M. Rodde Memorial Building

Fund. (The Rodde Center was an early Chicago LGBTQ community center, the forerunner to the Center on Halsted.) Mr. Football Hero also received a color television.

Man's Country used the same format for softball as well as football. In a 1977 game at the Belmont Rock, the Man's Country team was pitted against ballplayers from the local gay social and fundraising organization, Lincoln Park Lagooners. The game was another fundraiser for the Pride Week festivities. That evening at Man's Country, a Mr. Baseball Hero was named. To earn the title, each contestant had exactly two hours to raise money. The gent who raised the most money received one hundred dollars, a year's pass to Man's Country, and the title of Mr. Baseball Hero.

The Mr. Man's Country contest was another event that brought capacity crowds to the bathhouse every February, with the proceeds from the evening donated to a designated charity. Oftentimes the money was donated to help fund the Rodde Center. The contest provided a night of fun and excitement. Guys came to cheer their friends and whistle for their favorites.

The legendary bathhouse also played an important role in the history of the International Mr. Leather Contest (IML). In the early years of the competition, Man's Country was an official part of the contest. The IML meet and greets with the contestants and judges were held at Man's Country. The interview portion of the contest was frequently held there as was the meet and greet with the public.

After the contest was over, Man's Country was the site of the Black and Blue Ball, the huge dance party at the end of IML weekend. The event started in the early 1980s as "a dance party and orgy" held at the bathhouse. Most of those in town for IML were eager to cap the weekend with some serious revelry. At the dance, the newly crowned International Mr. Leather was declared King of the Black and Blue Ball—symbolically ruling over the orgy/dance party. The event was a huge success and quickly outgrew the Music Hall capacity before moving to larger venues.

A group of gay cloggers out of Atlanta, the Buffalo Chips, danced at one of the leather parties at Man's Country, entertaining alongside Judy Tenuta and her accordion. Clogger Jim Blythe recalled, "We filled up the Music Hall and we were so popular that Chuck brought us back a year later. We wore jeans and either our red western shirts with fringe, or a white shirt with a red bandana around our necks. We did three or four numbers. The sound was deafening—twelve cloggers on the floor and our music had to be loud to hear it over the clogging."

"I remember the dance floor at the Black and Blue at Man's Country," said Jon Krongaard. "It was filled to capacity. I couldn't believe the place didn't collapse. If you were downstairs at the Eagle, the speakers on the ceiling were shaking."

"The Black and Blue Ball was the best," said Wayne Hussey. "I remember dancing on one of those risers, looking out and seeing all those hot leathermen. Those parties were over the top. IML weekend was almost over and everyone could relax, and have fun. There was a sense of camaraderie. Nobody was judging. You could do what you wanted and be who you wanted. It was a real freedom. At one of those parties I ate Jeff Stryker's ass! He was on stage dancing and when he bent over a friend and I started eating his ass on stage."

Man's Country's connection to the community wasn't all big parties and fundraisers. Sometimes the connection ran deeper and was more personal. In a 1985 column, Jon-Henri Damski praised the Man's Country staff. "I have known them to send flowers to their 'anonymous customers' when they were in the hospital." (*Windy City Times*, 1985).

For many gay folks, especially those rejected by their biological families, the holidays can sometimes be difficult. In an attempt to make the holidays a little less isolating, Thanksgiving and Christmas dinner was held on-site at Man's Country for those with nowhere to go. Chuck and Dom usually served the meal. In later years, Man's Country also added a spaghetti night on Tuesdays.

Around the holidays, the Man's Country Players often did a production that featured much of the staff. The fun and festive holiday show came with plenty of skin and raunchiness. The holiday pageant was silly and sexy, but mostly the show was a celebration of being together.

"In 1976, we did *Holidaze on Ice*," recalled Gary Chichester. "It starred Wanda Lust and the Man's Country Players. For the ice we got big interlocking pieces of Lucite and coated them with silicone spray, so it was slippery like ice. Then we created a large rink by raising that coated surface up from the dance floor. We performed the show two nights.

There were all sorts of acts. Some of the guys were the seven dwarfs and sang, "Hi Ho, Ho Ho." The first night of the show it worked, probably because of all the drugs we were on. The second night the show fell apart for the same reason. But we had fun."

For members looking for a change of scenery, there were even several bathhouse outings. Man's Country Night at the Races was an event open for members willing to pay the twenty dollars for a bus trip to Maywood Park to make a few bets and enjoy some harness horse racing. Champagne was served on the chartered coach bus. Dinner was served in the "terraced dining room" of the Silk'n Sulky. At the track, the attendees made some bets, but the real reason for the road trip was to celebrate that the 6th feature race at Maywood Park that day was named after Man's Country.

There were other bathhouse outings as well. Bette Midler was just dipping her mermaid fin into the mainstream when a number of folks at Man's Country decided to go see her at the Auditorium. The group from Man's Country got twenty front row seats. Arriving in trench coats, the group sat quietly until Midler came on. The moment she stepped on stage, the group stood up and removed their coats. Underneath, all twenty men wore nothing but towels. Midler laughed and offered a smile, "Oh, it feels like I'm home."

In 1976, Man's Country was sent invitations from the Chicago Film Festival for a private showing of *The Ritz* starring Rita Moreno. The event was being held on the far Northwest side of the city. Once again, the Man's Country contingent dressed for the occasion, arriving in trench coats with only towels and locker keys underneath.

There were on-site events like Casino Night, "an evening of fun and games, prizes and laughter." Like many of the gay bars in the pre-VCR era, Man's Country had a Movie Night. At the bathhouse, movie night was Sunday night. The showings on the big screen in the Music Hall were a popular way to come down from or extend the weekend. Watching movies together in the Music Hall was a simple and effective way for members to have a shared group experience.

"The bathhouse got their copies of the films from the Rainbow Society for the Deaf." Chichester added, "They were 16mm because they would be close-captioned. Wanda loved to make the showing as big of a production as she could. She introduced the movie and often had a skit or number at the start to tie-in with the film."

The movie night bill might be everything from *Bedknobs and Broomsticks* to *The Maltese Falcon*. Additional Sunday showings included *The Wild One, Imitation of Life, Mary Queen of Scots, Madame X, Mary Poppins, Ryan's Daughter, The Happy Hooker, Hercules, Mildred Pierce, Bringing Up Baby, All About Eve,* and *Now, Voyager.*

Man's Country even had a Salute to the MGM Musicals, which were five consecutive Sundays of double features: *On the Town* and *Singing in the Rain, Meet Me in St. Louis* and *Showboat, Seven Brides for Seven Brothers* and *The Wizard of Oz, Million Dollar Mermaid,* and *Gigi,* and *Easter Parade* and *The Bells Are Ringing.*

Chichester and Wanda even experimented with 8mm filmmaking. "We had a porn film festival," said Chichester. "We spliced 8mm movies and made it a music video with different songs. There was one porn scene with two guys working on a house and so we played a Carpenters song. And then we would have another porn clip that tied to the music. The soundtrack was silly like that. People loved it."

As a personal touch, Man's Country members were given free admission with a guest on their birthdays. The bathhouse had plenty of other door specials as well, most of them with a hefty discount. There was Buddy Night, bring a buddy and get in half price; Jockstrap Night, present a jockstrap at check-in and get a locker for half price. There was Club Night, members wearing motorcycle club patches got a locker for half price; Founder's Night, a free locker to those with membership from opening night. College Night was half price admission with a valid student ID. Three Dollar Night meant all lockers and rooms were three bucks. The three-dollar amount was in reference to antiquated phrase, Queer as a Three Dollar Bill.

Man's Country also had a big presence in the Chicago Pride Parade. Chichester recalled an especially memorable float the staff created. "It was wonderful. It was a scroll with the Oscar Wilde quote, 'The Love That Dare Not Speak Its Name.' That was a great old school float— flatbed chicken wire, plywood, paper mache, and tissue paper float."

In 1976, Wanda Lust was widely photographed atop the Man's Country's Bicentennial Pride float. As Lady Liberty, Wanda wore the sunburst headpiece on her flaming red hair, and a red toga adorned with stars draped over her. In Wanda's upraised arm, she held a dildo instead of a torch. For the tablet Lady Liberty cradled in her other arm, Wanda held a laminated menu from her favorite diner. Another year, Wanda was at the top of the float in an enormous hoopskirt and a feathered headdress. The following year, Wanda radiated golden era Hollywood glamour in a silver gown.

Renslow recalled another Pride Parade float entry. "One time we did a concentration camp. We had a flatbed with barbed wire around the edges and the prisoners were leathermen. It was for the Pink Triangle, *Never Again* movement. I think it was when they were talking about putting people with HIV in those containment camps. (*Leatherman*, 2011).

Man's Country was more than just a bathhouse a several reasons, but this 1980 write-up in *Drummer Magazine*, #38 made the real reason clear. "A list of the facilities of Man's Country reads less like a description of a baths than like a brochure for a mythical fantasy land somewhere around the corner from Nirvana; a full-sized and stunningly equipped disco; a large private sundeck; numerous private rooms; a couple 'special' private rooms for leathermen; a large full stocked snack bar; a giant video-screening room; and a distinctly dungeon-like shower/whirlpool area. Those chains in the whirlpool get as much use as the on-off knobs on the showers."

The *Drummer* piece continued, "But the main attraction is the men—at any hour of any day of the week, Man's Country is heavily populated with Chicago's hottest, horniest hunks. You don't come here to crash—you come for steamy, sweaty Chicago-style action. Or else."

Chapter Eight

And then, paradise vanished. In June 1981, the Center for Disease Control announced that five men in Los Angeles had been diagnosed with a rare type of pneumonia.

In Chicago, the initial impact of AIDS was felt later than on the coasts. In a 1995 interview with Jack Rinella, the late AIDS activist Tom Domkowski remarked, "[AIDS] didn't take hold here in Chicago until two years later. It really didn't start hitting until 1983 when people started to know [people getting sick]. Sudsy was among the first group. It's like, 'Gosh, Sudsy looks great. He's on a diet or something.' He had that three-month period where he looked great and then he went down hill. And then it was like, something's wrong with this, something that the people aren't telling us about this whole thing. I think, mid 1984, late 1984 before people really started to talk about it."

Gay retiree GL recalled, "Overnight the world went from a place of sexual freedom to sexual hell. Nobody wanted to talk about it, and nobody wanted to think about it. But it was hard to think about anything else. That was early on, when it was still called GRID. Everyone thought it was some sort of poppers cancer."

In a 1985 column, Jon-Henri Damski wrote about how the Man's Country scene had changed. "I returned to Man's Country on a Saturday night—one of their better ones, I hear—and only 80 guys were there. Three guys were in the Snack Bar when I arrived, and four guys on the dance floor."

Damski continued, "Man's Country has sunk. Not just because of AIDS, but more because they haven't kept pace with even their local competitors. Comparing prices, rooms, beds, sheets, pillows, tiles in the steam room, and water in the whirlpools, I would say that they have not kept pace in basics with [Chicago bathhouses] the Unicorn and CHAPS.

They have not put videos into their private rooms. Not all of their showers and all of their toilets were in working order the night I was there. I had to wait ten minutes for a towel. With business down, their staff is down. They couldn't keep up with the midnight 'rush.'

"Most shocking to me," added Damski, "that night was that the orgy room was open, dark, full, and active just as in the past. They are not yet following the guidelines, like Unicorn and Club [Baths] Chicago, of Independent Gay Health Clubs (Man's Country was an original member of IGHC but has since discontinued their membership). (Damski, "Report on the Bathhouses in Chicago," *Windy City Times*, 1985).

As evidenced in Damski's column, "gay cancer" or GRID (Gay Related Immune Disease) had dire effects on the community and on Man's Country. Once the means of transmission was determined, Chuck closed the orgy room, the glory holes, and any area where there could be wide-open promiscuous sex. "I didn't give out condoms at the time because we still didn't know about that, but as soon as we found out condoms could stop it, I immediately started giving them out." (*Leatherman*, 2011).

In October 1985, New York health officials voted to close "homosexual bathhouses" and other gay gathering places where high-risk sexual activity occurred. Soon after the ruling, Los Angeles and San Francisco officials voted to shutter their gay bathhouses as well.

When the bathhouses began closing in New York and San Francisco, Chuck said he thought the Health Department here was going to Man's Country as well. "The guy who came out got the commissioner to come out and he went through it. I unlocked the door and explained this was the orgy room and this was where the glory holes were. I explained it all to him and he said, 'I'd rather have people in here where it's safer than out in the parks spreading the disease.' He never bothered me again."

In a 2011 *Windy City Times* piece 'AIDS: The Plague Years,' Chicago publisher Tracy Baim wrote, "In Chicago, the bathhouse controversy never reached the same crescendo—or outcome—as the closing of the baths in San Francisco. Chicagoans connected with the political establishment made it clear that unsafe sex was going on in many places, and that the goal was to educate men wherever they were—and that bathhouses were safer than parks and other cruising areas, because condoms could be handed out and safer-sex information posted."

Following the New York bathhouse ruling, in an editorial from October 19th, 1985, *The New York Times* also disapproved of the closings, believing the bathhouses were "useful locations for the dissemination of educational materials regarding AIDS."

Some of the additional concerns raised over the bathhouse closings were expressed in the 1985 *Windy City Times* editorial, *Don't Close the Baths.* The editorial echoed the sentiment that closing the bathhouses meant closing potential sites for AIDS education and condom distribution but touched upon other points as well. "What is troubling is the fact that it appears that closing bathhouses in an attempt to control "promiscuous" sexual activity could lead to other measures, ones that may affect the lives of the approximate 95% of the population that does not frequent such establishments in the first place."

The editorial continued, "Can we expect the state (in this case, perhaps Illinois) to attempt to close places where gays simply tend to meet—like bars? If so, who will decide which locations promote "potentially" dangerous forms of conduct and which don't? Is the closing of bathhouses the first round of ammunition loaded in an attempt to force the gay community into controlled, in not eventually quarantined, behavior?

"There are some very fine lines being drawn here, and there is little evidence (based on precedent) to suggest otherwise, particularly when one looks at this country's basic homophobic attitudes and the general lack of compassion and knowledge on the part of vociferous anti-gay leaders, political, and otherwise.

"The fact is that people have diseases, not places. And while some places have attracted a minority of gay people seeking to (possibly) engage in what has turned out to be life-threatening forms of behavior, most places haven't. Should the future freedom of hundreds of thousands of gays be at risk for that of a few thousand?

"The answer is no, particularly in light of telling evidence of late which indicates a substantial drop (even up to 75 percent) in recorded instances of venereal diseases among gays. This drop indicates that most gays have already significantly altered their behavioral patterns.

"It is also important to remember that due to the lengthy incubation period for AIDS, those people being diagnosed as having the disease today were infected at a time when little knowledge concerning the disease and its method of transmission was available. Consequently, those dying of AIDS today did not have the same choices open to them which uninfected individuals do now.

"What we need today is more educational outlets, a more sympathetic "straight" press, and increased government appropriations. We do not need government authorities attempting to control individual behavior in arbitrary, unproductive ways. The gay community has already suffered the most, and has made enormous strides in helping people to learn how to protect themselves and their loved ones. Closing bathhouses is not the answer. It is not a good answer at all."

In a January 1986, Eric Zorn reported for the *Chicago Tribune*, "Neither the AIDS Activities Office of the Chicago Department of Health nor the Illinois Department of Health have tried to close or regulate the bathhouses. And sponsors of the recently drafted AIDS-control legislation in the Illinois House of Representatives said they will not call for the closing of bathhouses."

The Zorn piece continued, "'Our anecdotal evidence shows that men who still go to the baths have changed their behavior,' said William Mannion, director of health education for the AIDS Project at the gay-oriented Howard Brown Memorial Clinic. He said the clinic does not favor closing bathhouses, because they provide 'an avenue to reach people who really need to be reached: the men who engage in a lot of sex and men who are married or closeted.'"

In 1987, the bathhouse issue resurfaced with the publication of *And the Band Played On: Politics, People, and the AIDS Epidemic* by Randy Shilts. Chuck was furious that the book strongly implied that Man's Country remained open because he "published the local gay paper and carried substantial weight in gay Democratic politics."

Chuck had published *Gay Life* newspaper. He stepped in and bought the paper when the paper was on the brink of going under. But *Gay Life* was no longer in business. The paper went out of business in 1986, leaving the *Windy City Times* and *Gay Chicago*.

In *Leatherman*, Chuck addressed the additional claims. "He [Shilts] said I kept the bathhouse open on account of my political pull, which was absolutely wrong. I had political pull, but that was not the reason I stayed open. I showed that a bathhouse could actually help teach about safe sex. The Health Department administrator was very progressive and Man's Country had a reputation with on-site STD testing and the VD van for gonorrhea and syphilis and all that."

When the tubs in other cities closed abruptly, with nothing but a padlocked front door and a public health notice, it was terrifying for patrons, especially at a time when there was little information aside from updated death statistics. President Reagan had yet to mention the AIDS virus. That would take him five years—sixty months. The Reagan administration, with close ties to the religious right, had also cut funding for things like public health and sex education, mental health counseling, and additional social service programs. The sudden closure of the bathhouses also came following a systematic dismantling of resources.

Dean Ogren applauded Chuck's decision. "It was a place to educate and get a message out to a community of people who were stretched and dying and looking for support. Man's Country was a community center for a lot of people. It was not just a sex club—it was a social center and a social outlet. It was always part that, and people needed that."

A significant percentage of those in the community had a different opinion and felt that Chicago should have followed suit and closed its bathhouses. "Absolutely," said one member. "All three of the bathhouses in town at the time should have closed to minimize exposure to HIV."

Once safer sex guidelines were established, safe sex information, posters, and signage took a prominent place at Man's Country. Posted on the wall at the entry to the club was the sign, NO CONDOM = NO F***. Baskets of condoms were located throughout the bathhouse complex. In addition, members were given a condom, along with a key and towel, at check-in.

As reported by Eric Zorn for the *Chicago Tribune* in January 1986, "Signs on almost every wall caution against sexual activity that involves the exchange of bodily fluids, specifically oral and anal sex. Doctors think such activity spreads the AIDS virus. The signs also urge the use of condoms. Desk clerks at Man's Country distribute about 300 free condoms a week, club officials said."

Similar to the steps taken for STD/STI testing a decade earlier, Man's Country developed a schedule and system for on-site HIV testing. TPAN (Test Positive Aware Network) set up a testing area from 9PM—12AM on Wednesdays. Howard Brown came to Man's Country and made free anonymous testing available for a three hour stretch every other Thursday.

"I was at Howard Brown from 2009-2014," said Keven Cates, MD. "I was young and we did intermittent outreach at local bars, clubs, and bathhouses. We distributed condoms, lube, and some light information—pamphlets. We also did on-site HIV and STD testing. I remember at Man's Country we did that in the Sling Room and the condom table was in the open area outside the Music Hall. I had no idea what to expect. The men there were very nice, very chatty. They seemed to genuinely appreciate our presence. We did pre and post-test counseling. We delivered HIV results on-site and if those came back positive, we were there to help the person decide on their next step. That real life experience certainly has informed my work. I am a better doctor today for having done that and had that experience."

Man's Country hosted workshops on safer sex and ways to enhance the experience while helping men protect themselves and their partners from HIV. The bathhouse also became a central meeting place for several social/sexual groups that practiced safer forms of sex, such as the Windy City Jacks.

In 1985 Jon-Henri Damski wrote of a Man's Country safe-sex encounter after perusing the preferences on the board in the bathroom. "Two items in chalk surprised me: 'Fistaval in 44' and 'JO 21.'" Damski headed for JO 21.

The column continued, "... What a sight! His door was open as his mind, his light was on full, and he was treating himself very well. I thought I recognized him as a former Mr. from Windy City a few years back. 'Mr. Loading Zone.' Blonde hunk. Clean fresh white jock strap. Large size. Seductive eyes. The hottest 'Mr.' in the place.

"After passing by his room several times, I took a stumbling step towards coming in his room. He turned his eyes away. His signal was clear. He didn't want me in his room.

"Routine bathhouse rejection. In the past I could have just gone on.

"But we are living in different times. I paced up and down his hall, trying to summon up courage to tell him what I thought.

"Soon he got down and came out of his room. I met him in the hall.

"'You are the best one here tonight, I really appreciate your safe scene. Your full light JO room turned me on more than the dark Orgy Room." (*Windy City Times*, 1985).

Chapter Nine

By 1985 news of AIDS was everywhere and attendance at Man's Country plummeted. The enormity of Man's Country made the place seem even emptier. Despite the personal losses Chuck suffered throughout this period, he realized that he needed to do something with the extra space to save his business. The solution was to reconfigure the building itself. A large portion of the bathhouse remained Man's Country, but the Music Hall and its lobby area were closed off as well as the area on the level directly below. The rear of the bathhouse on those two floors was soon transformed into Chicago's hottest new dance club.

The Bistro had been an enormously popular Chicago gay disco. Opening in 1973, it was an immediate sensation. Often called the "Studio 54 of the Midwest," the Bistro actually predated the iconic New York disco by four years. The Bistro was outrageous. Though a gay bar, the Bistro's uninhibited and celebratory atmosphere attracted celebrities and local glitterati. The Bistro was written about in *the Chicago Tribune*, *Sun-Times*, and *the Chicago Daily News*. The success of the disco was due in large part to the magnetic personality of its owner, Eddie Dugan. After the original Bistro closed in 1982, Dugan opened another club, Paradise, but that closed after four years.

In 1986, Chuck Renslow and Eddie Dugan decided to open a new Bistro. Eddie was deeply involved in the initial plans, but his health was rapidly deteriorating. "Eddie and Chuck had been friends for years," explained Dugan's right-hand man, TL Noble. "Ever since their bars [the Gold Coast and the Bistro] were a block from each other. After Eddie left Paradise, Chuck said he had a space. Lou DiVito, the head DJ at the Bistro, Eddie, and I got together and Lou did the blueprints."

Chuck's partner in Bistro Too, and in life, Ron Ehemann, captured a bit of the planning process. "Eddie and Chuck would come and then would look at the model and say, 'No we need to move this here or do that.'"

"Then Eddie got very sick," said Noble. "He was dying and Chuck went to see him. Eddie told him that he had taught me everything. That was how I got involved. By then, Lou had left the bar scene. He helped with the blueprints and later he helped with some graphics, but he was through with being a DJ in the clubs. When we opened, Lou's protégé, Jeff Berry, came in as the DJ."

Eddie Dugan died of AIDS in 1987, a few months before the opening of the revamped Bistro, which by then was called Bistro Too. In homage to Eddie and the Bistro, the neon word, *Boogie,* was added to the décor. Although the font was different, the neon sign was reminiscent of the one that hung on the wall all nine years the original Bistro was in business.

The Bistro had also used a certain shade of dark green as a recurring motif in the décor, regardless of several overhauls of the Bistro, some of the dark green remained. The group decided to choose a signature color for Bistro Too as well. "I think it was TL Noble's idea to have a print instead," recalled Ron Ehemann. "So a zebra print was used. A zebra pattern appeared inside the club on benches and chairs."

The zebra pattern was on the club's envelopes and advertising. An enormous zebra-patterned mural was painted on the southern wall of Man's Country with an arrow pointing down the alley to the Bistro Too entrance. "I painted that zebra mural myself," recalled TL Noble. "That was like free advertising space. The wall took me almost a week to paint. I did it freehand on brick with enamel paint. I didn't use a stencil. Once people saw that zebra pattern and the arrow, they knew Bistro Too was down the alley."

Bistro Too also used the zebra theme for a memorable Pride Parade float. "It was Cinderella's carriage," said Ehemann. "Only she was being pulled by two fiberglass zebras, originally horses—but we painted them as zebras. And the tagline on the float was, If You Have To Be Home By Midnight, Don't Bother."

"I was working as the editor of *Gay Chicago* when they were converting the space," said Rick Karlin. "TL Noble gave me a tour. The dance floor was the Music Hall, which had those big pillows around the sides. When I was getting the tour from TL, I pointed to a place on the floor and said, 'There should be a star there. That's where I had my first orgy.' And TL stopped and said, 'If we gave out stars for that, this floor would be littered with them.'"

Noble brought several ideas to the club. "I wanted the same music downstairs and upstairs. People needed to hear music in the main bar and get directly to the dance floor. That was when they put in the spiral staircase. Eddie was always big on a club's traffic pattern. Chuck agreed. A bar has to flow so people can cruise, get to the bathroom, the dance floor, and the bar."

Ehemann added, "We burned through three chainsaws trying to get through this incredibly solid floor of this former lodge to put in the spiral staircase."

"I was working at Take One," said Scott Taylor, "when I heard Eddie and Chuck were opening a new club. I had worked at Bistro and at Paradise. I was excited about the size of the place and the dance floor. I ended up working there. I was head bartender at the start, and I was there until it closed. Once the upstairs bar opened off the dance floor—that was my bar. Anyplace I've worked I have wanted the dance bar. Gary Boots was the main guy behind the bar in the game room."

Though not yet open to the public, Bistro Too had a test run in 1987 when Chuck chose the club as the venue for the LGBTQ social event of the season, the annual White Party. Every August, Chuck hosted the event. The White Parties were over the top. Folks went all-out to attend, dressing in their finest, most outrageous, and often sexiest, all white attire.

To prepare the unfinished place for the upcoming party, Chuck had the second floor of Bistro Too spray-painted white—everything from walls to doorknobs. Given the enormous turnout standard at most of the White Parties, Chuck was concerned that the Bistro Too would be too small to handle the crowd, so he recruited the nearby bars, Different Strokes and Clark's on Clark, to help with the overflow. As a way to visually connect the three venues with the White Party, the streetlight poles along that stretch of Clark Street outside the three participating bars (Bistro Too, Clark's on Clark, and Different Strokes) were decorated to be white palm trees.

The official Grand Opening of Bistro Too happened two months later, October 23rd and 24th, 1987. At the celebratory event the champagne flowed, and toasts were made to the return of the great Chicago nightclub, to the original Bistro, to Eddie, and to the future success of Bistro Too.

Steve Dale wrote of the club opening in the November 8th, 1987 issue of the *Chicago Tribune*: "General Manager and lighting designer TL Noble called the décor of Bistro Too as Deco-Tec—a combination of art deco and 'high tech.' The main barroom on the first floor was encircled by multi-colored neon lights. Ask the bartender to point out the high-frequency electrostatic generator. This space-age gadget emits a high-pitched sound that somehow causes the neon lights at the center of the bar to shine. Also at the center of the bar eerie plasma balls (those circular-shaped lights that appear to have lightning bolts inside) strike to the beat of the music videos shown on four screens. (There's always some type of slide show too.) If you hear a tune that you like, just walk up the winding staircase to the dance floor."

Dale continued, "If the main bar is 'Disco-Tec,' the dance room might be called 'Art-Tec.' On one side of the dance floor is a mural of the Chicago skyline; the other side features a mural of Lake Michigan, both by Chicago artist Octavio. A computer-programmed lighting system called Arc Lighting adds a touch of Hollywood to it all. There's also a stage; eventually the club intends to book local acts and occasional 'surprise' guests. And if you're looking for some relative quiet, there's a game room nearby. 'We are a high energy club,' says club owner Chuck Renslow, 'I challenge someone to come here and not have fun.'"

Ehemann added, "We got Roboscans, which were an intelligent lighting system that had been introduced by the band Genesis for their concerts. They were super-expensive. With a flipped switch a program would play and you could program the lights to change color or make the strobes go off or lights sweep the room and jump around or move in circles. It also had gobos, templates that moved in front of the light that could change it into different things—stars or beads or whatever."

"As general manager," said TL Noble. "I didn't stay in the office. I thought a bar manager should be on the floor making sure the customers have a good time. Another thing I told Chuck that he needed to change if he wanted to run a successful dance club. At his businesses, the bartenders were not supposed to drink. I told him that wouldn't work here. At a club the customers need to feel like it's one big party."

"I was so excited to launch that bar as house DJ," said Jeff Berry. "I had my light man there, Ray Van. It was a big deal. This place had robotic lights and no one had seen programmable lights at the time."

On the first floor of Bistro Too was the octagon-shaped main bar. The spiral staircase to the dance floor was in the southeast corner of the room. The main staircase was to the left of the entrance and led up to a game room, which was what much of the lobby of Man's Country's Music Hall had become. Off the game room was another bar that shared a wall with the dance bar in the old Music Hall. The dance bar was beneath the DJ booth.

"As the manager," said TL Noble. "I asked Chuck to build a room between those two bars. I wanted a room where there could be an ice machine and supplies for both bars. In a club on a busy night, no one has time to go downstairs for ice."

At Bistro Too the walls on the main floor were covered with video monitors screening strange and unusual clips from an array of sources that Ehemann discovered scouring video stores around town. "Sometimes, I recorded unusual clips on TV. The stranger the footage, the better," laughed Ehemann.

As part of the visual wizardry of the club, Bistro Too also projected still images. "We used lots of Chuck's vintage beefcake collection from Kris Studio," said Ehemann of the slides. "We also projected photos from old Chicago Pride Parades. Chuck had a huge collection of community images from the archives of *Gay Life* newspaper."

Bistro Too also started recording everything that happened in the club for potential use on the video walls. The archives of Bistro Too events contain rare footage of numerous acts and parties. The footage serves as a terrific time capsule to the edgy club scene of the late 1980s and early 1990s, where anything might happen.

With the screens, the monitors, and the projected images, the visual component was a big part of the Bistro Too experience. Ron and TL knew that for all that to work it was important to have an uninterrupted sight line in the club. So the lighting for the bar instead came from colored neon tubes beneath the white Plexiglas bar frame. "We didn't want anything hanging down," explained Noble. "Lou DiVito drew up the plans for the white milk glass with the neon inside." The same motif was used with the cocktail tables throughout the bar.

"We needed to show people that the staff was part of the good time," explained Noble. "With the TL Noble and Family Show, we basically worked the staff into a variety show. We did their make-up and had them rehearse. Sometimes I would have guest stars, like Bertha Butt came in and did a show. Kim Spaulding was always in the shows. Kim and I worked together at Bistro, at Paradise, and now at Bistro Too. He was so talented. He could do anything—dance, perform, drag, not drag—always sensational. We did lots of fun production numbers."

TL also recalled doing *Pink Cadillac* by Natalie Cole. "I told Chuck I wanted to bring a car on stage. Instead, we got the front of a pink Cadillac El Dorado. I did two spotlights as headlights aimed in different directions so they wouldn't be straight on at the crowd. Then I taped pieces of painted cardboard on the backdrop coming out from the front of the car to make it look like the front of the El Dorado had crashed through the wall. To introduce the song, we played the sound effect of a car accident, I tossed a smoke bomb underneath the car, the curtain opened, and I was sitting on the hood for the song. I considered myself more of a female imposter than anything. I was in drag, but I was always TL Noble doing my own version of a song."

Noble recalled another show, "We did *Vogue* with the Meatpackers as my backup dancers and all the girls got to pick their favorite character in the song to be. I remember that Jamma did Bette Davis in full *All About Eve* drag—and even used her real hair!"

"We had so much fun there," said Jim Meischner aka Jamma. "The shows were so wild—TL, Kim Spaulding, Shelley DeWinters, Tina Tec. Shelley and I never messed up our lip synch. TL always did her own thing with make-up and that hair we called the mushroom wig. Every month we tried to grab a bartender or bar back and put them in drag. I worked the coat check and made so much money there. On nights I had a show, I did coat check in drag, did the show, and came back to do coat check in drag. I remember the night Duran Duran walked into the club and freaked everyone out."

"I started going there was I was 19," said Angelique Munro, "when I was Teddy. I was a huge Grace Jones fan and heard this performer at Bistro Too did her. Seeing Tina Tec as Grace Jones live was life changing. She did *Love on Top of Love*—the song started, the curtain rose. She had on a black dress and her head was down. She was wearing this huge hat with a clock on it. I was over the moon. I was so excited."

Munro continued. "The first time I went there I was so green I didn't know what to order. I got in line and the man in front of me ordered a sea breeze. Because of that, I drank sea breezes for years. Mostly I went there to dance—Yaz, New Order, Black Box, Crystal Waters—I loved everything they played. Most nights I danced until they kicked me off the dance floor. Bistro Too was a nice introduction to gay club world, the dance floor world, and learning to accept my true self. My experience there was very positive."

"A friend told me about it," said Robert Castillo. "I kept going back because the music was great and I liked the diversity of the crowd, every color of the rainbow, everybody went there gay, lesbian, bi, straight, drag, everybody. It was very welcoming. I liked the camaraderie. They had pool and electronic games. The music was great. I remember hearing *Like a Prayer* by Madonna and *I Beg Your Pardon* by Kon Kan there for the first time. The first time a guy tried to pick me up was at Bistro Too. My friends and I always had fun just letting our hair down and dancing. Thursdays were dollar night. Many weekends my friends and I would be there Thursday, Friday, and Saturday."

"Probably 1988 or 1989 I started going to Bistro Too on dollar night," laughed Duke. "I loved the vibe, the crowd, the music, all of it. I loved to dance. My friends always joked that when I went out, I should wear loose fitting clothes because I'd be taking them off soon enough. At Bistro Too, I liked to work my way over to the pedestal on the right off the dance floor and get up there and dance. The third time or so that I did, somebody came over and said management wanted to talk to me. I thought, 'Oh shit.' But that's when I met Chuck and Ron. The next thing I knew I was dancing there on weekends. Dancing up there, it felt like I owned the place. I never felt so important."

"My favorite dance club on the North Side," said Malone Sizelove. "On Fridays I went to Normandy and on Saturdays I went to Bistro Too, because that's where all the Latin boys went. It was so much fun. I heard someone describe Bistro Too as Medusa's without the angst. It was a happy place. People were jovial. I met so many people there. Bistro Too was a terrific place to hang out and a great place to dance. There were carpeted platforms around the dance floor because people threw their coats on them when they danced."

"I loved the staff there," said David C. "One of my best friends, David, worked there. I hung out at his bar and he gave me free drinks. Once I went there, he was wearing a T-shirt and I was talking to him and I looked down and on his shirt was a picture of me passed out the week before. And he wore it all night. David was my first really close friend to die of AIDS."

"Bistro Too was eye opening for me," said Edwin A. "I remember going upstairs and just this mist of human sweat as I walked into the room. I remember the excitement of it all. Bistro Too was very accepting. It felt like a big party. It was just people enjoying the music and it was fabulous."

"At Bistro Too," said Jimmy D'Ambrosia. "like at Paradise, we had a code name for cocaine. *All My Children* was big at the time, so when we wanted to find out where to get cocaine we would say, 'Have you seen Erica?' And the person would say, 'Yes, she's right over there talking to Bob.' And you knew where to get it."

Robert Kimmons recalled dancing there. "I was dancing and a guy near me on the dance floor turned around and it was Jeff Stryker. And then we were dancing together. He leaned in and asked if I knew who he was and I said, 'I'm a gay man—of course I know who you are.'"

"I think I was twenty when I started going," said Robert Coddington. "I used an International Student ID that said I was twenty-three. Once in the door, I was in hog heaven. Two dance floors! Mostly I was excited to get into a community. You can't do much as a student. Going there was this explosion of freedom. We could dance, be together, be safe, and not get beaten up. I met so many people there. I gathered relationships I still have today from Bistro Too. I heard all kinds of music there. I was introduced to House Music there. I found mentors there who taught me the ropes—pickups, flirting, and gay etiquette. Meeting all sorts of people there made me accept a lot of variations of gay life because growing up in a small town in Indiana I tended to see it one way. Not after Bistro Too. I was exposed to everything there."

"My friends and I were Goths," explained Michael Nudo. "We started going to Bistro Too because they weren't too tough on carding. Dancing there exposed me to international pop and dance music, and extended remixes. We might go there and dance for six hours or until they kicked us off the dance floor. I found my tribe there. And it seemed like every night we were there was someone who would wipe out coming down those spiral stairs."

Photographer David Rustile was another patron who dodged the doorman. "We came into town to go to Medusa's, but I went there with mostly straight punk guys. We heard they were loose on carding at Bistro Too."

Like Rustile, Anthony Serranilla had been to Medusa's with friends when he discovered Bistro Too. "We tried Berlin, but got carded. We heard Bistro Too was easier, so we went and got in. Everything was so exciting. I loved the music they would spin. Bistro Too was the best place for dancing—they played Italian imports and new wave remixes. I would dance there from about eleven to one in the morning. At one the hardcore crowd came in. I usually cut out around then."

Serrannilla continued, "The fashion was another reason I went there. Seeing the looks I saw on MTV right there in front of me was big for me. I tried to top myself every week and elevate my style. I mixed women's clothing with men's clothing—very Morrissey meets Martika meets Jody Watley. Bistro Too was a place you could do that. The crowd was very eclectic. It was where I first saw drag queens and gay strippers. Bistro Too was where I met my first one-night stand and my first boyfriend."

Keeping things fresh was essential when it came to drawing the young queer club crowd. Changing the décor was one approach. "When we opened," said Ron Ehemann, "a cityscape mural by Octavio was on the walls of the dance floor. TL Noble was at the center of getting all that done. The original wall murals were done to look like you were on the rooftop of a skyscraper in Chicago, looking out at the city around you. Black light paint was incorporated as well—that would pop with a change of the lights. One time we changed it [the décor] to be Ancient Egypt. There were a few big changes. My favorite was the outer space theme. The makeover was something else Eddie Dugan had loved to do to keep the original Bistro fresh."

TL Noble added, "The Bistro Too dance floor was a big box and the walls were our blank canvas. The easiest way to change the look was to change the walls. We did that with the game room as well. We had the walls done in there with an outer space motif."

For the periodic redesigns, Bistro Too worked with a company called Prop Art, who helped do the murals and change the theme. For the Egyptian theme, the walls were changed. The stage was transformed into a pyramid with the top removed and replaced with a 3-D sphinx. "After that change I did *The Lion Sleeps Tonight,*" recalled TL Noble. "I had the Meatpackers carry me out in a sedan chair and I was wearing a zebra outfit and a Nefertiti headdress and then it segued into *Open Sesame* by Kool and the Gang."

Noble continued. "We were always doing something. It was fun. Another time we all did the *Thriller* zombie dance. We rehearsed for two and a half weeks with the entire staff to get that right. When we did it, the crowd loved it. The Meatpackers did the dance with us in loincloths."

Periodic "happenings" were another way to keep the club hot. These unannounced one-time events simply occurred. The strategy behind the happenings was simple, word of mouth. Keeping the club relevant and a popular spot meant people needed to keep talking about it...and people talk about the unexpected at a nightclub. Word of mouth was powerful, and FOMO was a popular force even before there was an acronym for the Fear of Missing Out. People didn't want to miss the appearance of the Bistro Too cash cannon, or a glitter explosion, or an unexpected performance, or a CD giveaway.

The club's resident hostess and house comic, Memory Lane, was another reason for the club's success. Absurd, avant-garde, and a real sweetheart, Memory often wore a nurse's outfit and two pairs of glasses—one pair she wore and the other hung on a chain to her enormous tits. Memory performed at the bar and emceed. She also circled the dance floor, wheeling a hospital fluids rack and selling shots out of an IV bag.

TL Noble talked about how Memory Lane started. "I went to Chuck with an idea of having her selling shots out of an IV bag. If he could see that having Memory Lane at the bar would help sell liquor, he would be on board. Memory Lane became the club emcee. I like to perform, but I don't necessarily like to speak into a microphone. The shows ran better with Memory Lane as the emcee. Then I found out about Memory's skill on the piano and the lounge singing and we had our warm up for the club."

At Bistro big-ticket events, like the Boy George or Divine concerts, Memory Lane also took Polaroids. Lane sold the instant photos of folks at the event for a few dollars and a tip. If you paid for the picture, Lane slipped the Polaroid into a nice cardboard souvenir sleeve stamped with her name and contact information. It was a nice souvenir from the evening.

"Memory Lane was such a lovely queen," added Robert Coddington. "She protected me. She befriended me early on. She was caring and sweet, witty and had really wonderful stage banter—and those big tits. Memory was nurturing. Before that, I was scared of queens. Not after. Memory was another great mentor."

Duke recalled, "One night I was dancing up on my pedestal and looked over and Memory shook her tits at me, and I jumped off the platform and ran over and buried my face in them. That was my first dollar Thursday at Bistro Too. And all I could think was, that place was fun, I want to go back."

Michael Nudo echoed the sentiments. "She really was a mother figure for some of us younger partiers, but at the same time she was also this wild Pop Art creation."

As a mentor to many of the younger club goers, Memory Lane was also a safe sex education activist. Memory Lane made and was the executive producer of the music video, *Condoms Are a Girl's Best Friend*, which was filmed in the Uptown Theater. The video debuted at Bistro Too. The video was produced, directed, and shot by Eric C. Kay. The project benefited the Reimer Foundation, which provided free condoms for dozens of bars and bathhouses in the area, in addition to safer sex promotional materials.

"My favorite part of the shows was when Memory Lane would sing in her own voice—beautiful," said Jim Meischner. "I did make-up and costumes for her videos. In *Condoms Are a Girl's Best Friend* I am a muscleman in black leather. I also worked with Memory on her video *Boobs* which we shot at Big Chicks."

In 1992, *Gay Chicago* gave a brief profile of the popular nightlife personality. "Memory Lane is the creation of Dean [Allrick] and is a regular entertainer at many local benefits and clubs. ... Memory Lane is not quite a drag queen and certainly not a female impersonator. Memory is really a female comic that shares a body (and a great deal of man-made fibers) with [Allrick]. The closest equivalent would be Phyllis Diller."

Memory Lane was a popular emcee and comic throughout the Midwest. During her time at Bistro Too, Lane also appeared in shows, hosted events, and took part in numerous AIDS fundraisers at Bistro Too as well as at other LGBTQ venues of the era such as Christopher Street, Vortex, Sidetrack, and Cairo.

Bistro Too was the site of numerous AIDS benefits for a myriad of AIDS organizations—Stop AIDS Chicago, The Names Project, Chicago House, the Reimer Foundation, Open Hand, and more. In 1991, Bistro Too had a big fundraising event to raise money to sponsor Memory Lane in the AIDS Walk. The "Sponsor Memory Lane in the AIDS Walk" campaign raised a great deal of money. The slogan was simple, "Help Memory Lane Carry Her Titties Across the City."

The club also hosted some amazing queer entertainment. Boy George, Divine, and the Village People all performed on the stage at Bistro Too. "Divine packed the place—I think we had 1,300 people for Divine," added Ehemann. Following his performance at Bistro Too on February 19th, Divine flew to LA for meetings about a recurring role in the TV series *Married With Children*. Divine died of an enlarged heart on March 7th. Sadly, Divine's performance at Bistro Too was one of his final club appearances.

In 1987, the Village People celebrated their 10th anniversary with a reunion at Bistro Too. The place was packed, and they played all their greatest hits—including "YMCA," "Macho Man," "In the Navy," and "Go West." The groundbreaking gay group even chose the evening to debut their new song, "Chicago Nights."

"In those days so many acts did New York, LA, San Francisco, and Fort Lauderdale," said TL Noble. "I wanted to make them remember Chicago. I decorated the dressing room. I made sure someone picked them up at the airport. I saw they were comfortable in town. I ran the rehearsal—coordinated the lights, was at sound check. I did everything I could to make the performers want to return."

The roster of talent that visited the club was impressive. Bistro Too hosted the talents of Thelma Houston, the Manhattan Transfer, Linda Clifford, Paul Parker, high-energy dance music favorite Viola "If You Could Read My Mind" Wills, and the company from *Porgy and Bess*. Evelyn Thomas, Promise Circle, Hazell Dean, and Odessa Brown played to the Bistro Too crowd as well.

Pamala Stanley played the Bistro Too. Noble knew her from when she performed at Paradise. "Fans loved her. She was one of the few acts who liked having dance remixes of their songs playing while they entertained. She was smart. During the long musical segments, she twirled these colorful hand fans [called 'fanning']. The crowd loved it."

Eventually, Bistro Too even had a troupe of male dancers, the Chicago Meatpackers. The group began in late 1990 when Tyler Adair arrived from Milwaukee and approached Chuck about being a regular dancer at the club. Chuck said if Adair found three other dancers, he would consider it. The rest is history. The original four were Adair (founder and captain), Mark Paxton, Beau Beaumont, and Tony Varone.

"They were a hit from the start," said Ehemann. "After a few weeks, we realized people wanted to see different dancers, so we started touring the group and expanded to a couple dozen dancers so there would be different dancers at Bistro Too as well." The Meatpackers, who stripped down to thongs, toured from Minneapolis to Fort Lauderdale and from Topeka to Pittsburgh. Some configuration of the group performed at Bistro Too on Friday and Saturday nights as well.

"I photographed the Meatpackers for *Gay Chicago* a few times," recalled Spike. "They were nice guys. They didn't party too much, like a lot of strippers. They were gorgeous and a good crew."

Camaraderie of staff was key to Noble's management style. "I wanted everyone on staff to feel they were a part of the place—because they were. When we redid the entrance area between the main bar and the main stairs. I put a tarp on the carpet and painted that entire entry black—walls, coat check door, all of it. Then, I got cans of the three original Bistro Too colors—purple, pink, and turquoise. Then I taught each of the staff to splatter paint each of the colors in one direction. The colors were so vibrant against the black that it gave the entrance a fluorescent feel, and everyone felt connected to the club they helped to paint. Doing that was also one of those times when I realized that abstract art had a definite place in the clubs."

From 1988 to 1991, Bistro Too was also the site of the Black and Blue Ball, the wild dance party held on the final night of IML weekend. The Village People returned to Bistro Too to headline the party the first year the Black and Blue Ball was at the club.

Israel Wright recalled one of those events. "Chuck gave everyone at the Black and Blue Ball a present and opened doors between the party and the bathhouse so we could all walk around and get off as much as we wanted."

"My favorite night as a DJ was the Black and Blue Ball," shared Jeff Berry. "I played everything I loved from old disco to high energy 1980s and 1990s stuff. The dance floor was packed all night with leathermen out there just having a good time. After I was done that night, these two leather daddies came up to me and said, 'Thanks for the best night of dancing in our entire lives.'"

Bistro Too was a fantastic venue for big gatherings and drew a sizeable crowd on the weekend. The greater concern was how to attract crowds on the slower nights of the week. The club was closed on Mondays and Tuesdays but filling the place on a Wednesday was not easy. "We needed 300 people minimum, or the place would look empty—500 looked good and 1,000 looked packed," said Ehemann. "Those numbers were hard to maintain."

One popular way to bring in crowds was using confetti cannons, which were sometimes filled with cash! For a while Wednesdays were Mondo Lezbo, a lesbian club night with dollar drink specials and lesbian entertainment such as stand-up comic, Deborah Daliege. In the early 1990s, Sunday nights became known as the Choice aka No Alcohol Sundays, with a five-dollar cover, high-energy dance music, and free coffee, juice, and soda.

The management tried two-stepping, Techno-Primitiv Nite, Video Night, Amateur Drag Shows, Shadow Dancing (behind a scrim), pizza parties, Salsa Night, Wet Jockey Shorts contests, and ballroom dance lessons. There were Stripper Saturdays where strippers were "intimately presented on the first floor." Bistro Too even had an amateur night for strippers, Strip Search, modeled after the television show *Star Search*.

In a 2001 interview, Steve "Killer" talked about Drag Queen Wrestling. "I started working in the bars in 1989…I was hired as a bar back and I went to a bartender…That was when drag queen wrestling came out, and that was a bunch of guys that got together, dressed up in drag and wrestled in the wrestling ring. We had a blast. That's how I got the name Killer. I'm Helen Killer, the blind wrestler. They would lead me on, then when I was in the ring, suddenly I could see! I wrestled against Tina, against the Bride of Doom, against Mad Mary Kay, and against Mildred Fierce…" (St Sukie de la Croix, 'Chicago Whispers,' *Windy City Times*, August 29th, 2001).

Memory Lane hosted the evening with ringside color commentary by TL Noble and "the mouth of the Midwest," Panama Red (aka John Sheridan). Noble recalled, "John Sheridan came to me with an idea for drag queen wrestling. He was into wrestling and wanted to make it a fun and campy event. We built the ring ourselves. At first there were injuries. When we first started, the ring just fell apart. At the start that was kind of the appeal. As it became more popular, we realized the ring had to be durable and we needed it to be able to be assembled and taken down quickly. And it could not have any hard or sharp edges. So it took some trial and error. We built the frame and then added a mattress and padding. Many of the wrestlers were bar staff and regulars. People really got involved. We gave them a theme song for when they came out, but they came up with their own personas. In the early matches, once things started, the first thing that happened was someone got their wig snatched off, so I also created these chin straps made out of pantyhose for the wrestlers to hold their wigs on."

Additional drag queen wrestlers included Goldirocks, Ninja Housewife, Diesel Debbie Lynn, Zula the Zebra Woman, Sister Mary Bruiser, Butch, Vicious Veronica, the Belmont Bag Lady, Juicy Butt, Gina Tay, Twisted Sister, and Misty Star, along with her manager, Vinnie Testosteroni.

Bistro Too tried Vampire Circus, an occult night advertised with the quote, "A darkened Sun, a brightened Moon, The Two shall reign as one." The evening featured professional tarot card readings, mood music, and more. For a while, one night of the week, the club became Klub Luna to lure the Goth/vampire crowd. Bands that played for Klub Luna include Dark Theatre, the Romanian Vampire Band, Amberyn Bridge, Killer Kitchen Utensils, and Fringe Element.

"When the crowd started to change," said Anthony Serranilla, "my friends and I stopped going. It started to get too rough. Fights were breaking out. A tougher crowd was going there."

"It was a great dance bar," added Scott Taylor, "but the neighborhood wasn't great. People were getting their cars broken into. We were having crowd problems. There were fights in the bar. The area was too rough, and that ruined business."

Bistro Too was a club that made a definite mark on the Chicago nightlife scene. The nightclub served as an alternative to the Halsted Street scene for five years before it closed in 1992. Ehemann summed up the demise of Bistro Too, "Eventually we lost the 'in' crowd because the 'in' crowd is always off to some newer place."

Chapter Ten

In September 1991, Chuck's partner in business and in life, Dom Orejudos died of AIDS at age 58. Over the past several years, Chuck had lost a steady stream of lovers and friends to the disease. The devastation and loss within Chicago's gay community was enormous. The leather community was hit even harder.

Although the fatality rate for the disease continued to climb, by 1992 much of the initial panic about HIV had subsided. There were now tools in place to navigate the new sexual landscape. Once scientists had discovered the means of HIV transmission, effective safer sex guidelines were established. Many gay men were learning that safer sex could be hot sex. AIDS was here to stay, at least for the time being. Once gay men accepted and became acclimated to this new reality, business at Man's Country began to gradually rebound.

With the closing of Bistro Too in 1992 and business at Man's Country on the upswing, Chuck wanted the Music Hall back as part of the bathhouse. As a result, the building underwent yet another drastic restructuring. The Music Hall and lobby area were once more reabsorbed into Man's Country.

With the closing of Bistro Too, the Chicago Meatpackers dissembled, but the guys stayed on to strip at Man's Country. Now that they were performing in a private club, the dancers stripped all the way.

Chuck explained the shift at Man's Country to having primarily strippers as entertainment. "...When we did that [earlier] we were the gay cabaret and people came here because they weren't welcome in other places. Today gay people are welcome all over—why come here when you can just go get a drink at some bar? Times have changed. Once the attitudes towards gay life, and especially leather men, everything started to change, then all our people started to go to regular bars. Two or three blocks from here there's a cabaret bar and they've got some top notch acts in there, and it's mixed, they get lesbians, gay men, straight people…they don't have to come here anymore. At a time, we were the only place for gay people to come." (Alex Godfrey, "Man's Country: A Man's a Club for Men," *Vice*, 2010).

As part of the new wave of entertainment, Man's Country featured dancers on the weekends—usually four dancers to open for a visiting porn star. The visiting XXX stars were not contractually required to ejaculate, though many of them did. One Man's Country member recalled the male dance revue at Man's Country as "a hard, hot, naked show."

"The turnout for those midnight stripper shows could be all over the place," recalled Ziggy Leroy. "Sometimes there were only a handful of people. It was uncomfortable when there wasn't a crowd. Sometimes there might be an audience of forty. The size of the audience was everything. When there was a good crowd there was such excitement. I remember there was a trans performer there one time and the crowd was huge. People were really excited to watch them perform."

"When the strippers were performing at Man's Country," explained Ron Ehemann, "Sarabia and Maria began to do the booking. Sarabia did the stage décor and was the show emcee and host. He appeared at the start of the show, during the show to announce each new dancer, and at the end."

"I came to Man's Country in 1996. I had a theater degree and background," said Sarabia. "I moved to Chicago and filled out an application at Man's Country. Chuck called me to interview. I thought I was interviewing for a custodial job so I explained to him that I'm very responsible, I show up on time for work, and things like that. At some point in the interview, Chuck stopped me and said, 'What position do you think you are interviewing for?' Actually, he was interviewing me as the new entertainment director. He showed me the theater [Music Hall] and I talked more about what I had done. He gave me a tiny budget, something like eighty dollars, and told me to dress up the stage. So I draped some fabric across the stage and glued broken mirror on the walls. Both Chuck and Ron liked what I did."

Sarabia continued, "When I started the shows were on their last legs. My budget got bigger and eventually we built an audience. We started rehearsing opening and closing numbers. We rehearsed the lights and cued the music. We changed the shows every week—new songs, new theme. One week the theme might be ropes, the next it might be Hawaii, or the Olympics. We built over one hundred sets in the years I ran the shows. The challenge was always, how do you draw an audience into the room to see a show when the alternative is to go have sex in another room."

To aid him in the ongoing task, Sarabia enlisted the help of college friend and theater colleague, Mari Otta. "I started two years after Sarabia. I started working the music and lights. I helped him make the sets and the costumes, helped with rehearsals, wrote out cues. Sometimes I even appeared in the productions—I might be a fairy in one production and then have a little bit in the next show as something else. Being in the show was my favorite part."

Sarabia added, "I wanted the audience to have a good time and enjoy the show. I loved hosting, going with whatever the audience was doing and winning them over. The pace was unbelievable—a different show every week. New theme, new songs, new costumes; and sometimes I had six costume changes in a show. Mari and I built so many sets. The sets would sometimes remain the same for two or three weeks. I remember one set was a frozen explosion with all sorts of things hung on invisible wires and then we marked on the floor the path the dancers had to walk to avoid the wires."

Porn actor Ricky Sinz recalled, "Man's Country used to have these bizarre productions. All sorts of crazy things...stuff you do not expect in that venue. One time for Halloween the stage was set up like a cemetery and Sarabia was a vampire and I was in a trance, he bit me, and laid me down on the stage. Then I rose, ripped my clothes off, and popped a load for the crowd. So yes, a jack-off show but with a twist." (*Leatherman*, 2011).

Overnight Man's Country became a popular venue for gay porn stars to dance. Hot House, Raging Stallion, Studio 2000—stars from many of the big studios at the time came to strip on the Music Hall stage. The dozens of gay porn stars to perform there included Ryan Idol, Matthew

Rush, Dino Phillips, Hans, Jason Adonis, Steve Rambo, Brian-Mark, Steve Cannon, Will Clark, Bobby Blake, Talvin DeMachio, Jake Andrews, Cole Tucker, Roman Heart, Erik Rhodes, and many more. To accommodate the visiting talent, one of the two Renslow apartments above 5025 N. Clark was turned into a "visiting porn star suite."

"Ron was smart about things," said Sarabia. "The night after the porn star arrived we would go film an interview with them at the suite. Then we would rehearse the next day. The night of the show there was a camera crew and simultaneously broadcast worldwide. So we were live streaming before anyone. Between dancers, I would come out or we would project parts of the interview we taped. The dancers could also burn DVDs from their performance and sell them."

Otta recalled the pace, "Doing two new shows a week over the years was such a wonderful and crazy experience. I was a theater major, both Sarabia and I were. We were working on creating shows—we were putting everything we learned in theater and dance into practice. At the end of every week we were exhausted."

Sarabia added, "But by the evening of the day after the show we usually would pick the theme for the next week. And then we would decide on the songs, and it would start all over again."

To keep the shows fresh, the three local male dancers in the revue were also rotated. Booking and scheduling dancers became another task that Otta assumed. "After booking them into Man's Country for a while, I started booking the dancers into other clubs as well. So, for a while I was also juggling this roster of about ninety dancers."

"When I first started at Man's Country it was strange going in there as a woman," recalled Otta. "But then I just said, fuck it. I thought, 'Okay, this is the most surreal experience I've had in my life. I am working in a gay male bathhouse. It was an education."

For the stripper shows, a shower stall was eventually installed on stage. "The shower kept fogging in the beginning," added Sarabia. "People couldn't see anything. We tried a defogging solution, but that didn't work. Eventually we just kept the door open and put six or seven towels on the floor to absorb the splash."

"I danced there every weekend for probably three years," said Duke. "I loved it. I would watch the top-liner and think, I want to be that guy.

Sometimes I was that guy, but you had to earn your stripes. I remember when LesBiGay Radio broadcast a show from there. Ron was on, since it was his show, Sarabia was on since he was the emcee, and I was on because I was their most reliable dancer. I loved it. I didn't care who watched. I danced for me. When I felt the music, it was like being in a hula-hoop and all that space inside was mine. Sarabia and I didn't always see eye to eye. Like any family we had our disagreements, but as a group we worked well together."

"It was the last grand bathhouse," added Sarabia. "There was nothing like putting on shows there with a proscenium stage for live performance. We took pride in that. The thing about those shows was, when it ended, it ended. The videos are all gone. That's the theater though, so much of the work is for a moment, and it goes. Working there was like a dream, but we can say we were a part of that—and there were so many magical nights."

In addition to the ongoing weekend shows, Man's Country hosted various special events. The second annual Grabby Awards for gay adult films were held in the Music Hall at Man's Country on May 29th, 1999. Although the Grabbys had been awarded the previous year, there had been no show. There was only the publication of a winner's list. Since Chicago was home to International Mr. Leather, Chuck suggested that the Grabbys could be added to the list of IML weekend activities. Chuck also offered free use of the Music Hall.

The late *GRAB* publisher Mark Nagel recalled, "When we were trying to get the Grabbys off the ground in 1998, Chuck offered free use of The Music Hall at Man's Country for the Awards ceremony. That was really essential for a new event." (*Leatherman*, 2011).

The Grabby Awards were a fundraiser for the free condom distribution group, the Reimer Foundation. The awards ceremony was co-hosted by popular Chicago performer Honey West and gay porn director Chi Chi LaRue. The event also featured a surprise appearance by the late Judy Tenuta. At the Grabbys that year, the gay porn Wall of Fame was also unveiled, which honored legends in the gay porn industry.

"That was the first year the Grabbys went live," recalled West. "Mark and Stacy asked me to do it. They were smart to have it in Chicago. If you had the porn awards in California it wasn't so interesting, but if you had it in Chicago—people were interested, they were intrigued and excited. The show sold out. That was also when I met Chi Chi. We have done the Grabby Awards every year since then."

Unlike the Gay Video News Awards (GayVNs), which were only open to industry and press, tickets to the Grabbys were available for public purchase. The event quickly sold out. Fans were eager to mingle with their favorite porn stars. The opening reception for the first two live Grabby Awards took place on the main floor with the event upstairs in the Music Hall. Guests who attended the event were also invited to stay and play at the bathhouse. Many accepted the offer.

West added, "At the first live show, the audience was clothed. There was some nudity on stage, but it was like naked Twister and it was in a private club, so that was an option. I had worked with strippers and male revues before, so for me this was just another gig. All the porn guys were from California. Chi Chi knew everybody, but I didn't know anybody— so I wasn't in awe of anyone."

"I was Trophy Boy that night," recalled Duke. "They told me I had to be nude to do it and I said sure. It was a wild evening. I know that at the end of the night, in the group photo Cole Tucker is down like he's blowing me."

Another attendee recalled the show. "I was there with my ride or die. I had a little too much to drink. Then there was an intermission, so I had a couple more drinks. Then, I think Chi Chi LaRue said, 'Anyone who thinks they have a big dick come to the stage,' and I ran up there. I think three guys did. I remember I yanked my pants down and then I fell and the next thing I knew Cole Tucker was eating my ass. After the show, Chi Chi gave me her card and said, 'if you want to do this give me call.' I never did, but it was nice to be asked."

After two years at Man's Country, the Grabbys outgrew the venue. By the third year of the live awards, the Grabby Awards ceremony was held at Circuit nightclub on N. Halsted in Lakeview.

Man's Country had been the venue for porn before. In 1996, legendary gay porn director John Travis shot the Studio 2000 XXX gay feature, *In Man's Country,* on location in the bathhouse. The film starred Sonny Markham, one of the Chicago Meatpackers. Additional cast members included Jake Andrews and Adam Rom. The gay adult feature is a time capsule of Man's Country interior at the time, with sex scenes shot in the locker room, the whirlpool grotto, and the Music Hall.

Writer and porn actor Scott O'Hara (1961-1998) called Man's Country his favorite bathhouse. He was a member in the early 1980s and often returned when he was in town. O'Hara found fame as "The Man with the Biggest Dick in San Francisco," the man with the HIV+ tattoo, a writer, and a queer sex activist. O'Hara also published the literary zine, *Steam: A Quarterly Journal for Men.*

In "A Tail in Three Cities" from the debut issue of *Steam* (Spring, 1993), O'Hara wrote a Man's Country review. "I was almost frightened off by the grunge that greeted me inside the lobby. Old, worn carpeting, redolent of piss, not the best of welcomes. I forged ahead, though, and ended up being glad: however run-down it may have become, some very interesting men still go there. You just wouldn't know it from the outside. The hot tub is still one of the largest & most 'atmospheric' I've ever been in (though the walls around it are now rather mildewed—or were they always like that, and I just never noticed?) and the steamroom is still 'the largest in the Midwest' (which doesn't mean a helluva lot if it's empty). The third floor disco, once accessible through Manscountry, has been sealed off and opened under separate management, with a separate entrance. (Talk about nostalgia!—I remember falling asleep on one of the pillows scattered around the dance floor, dreaming that I was being fucked, and waking up to discover that yes I was being fucked. Ah, those pushy Chicago boys...not that I protested.) There are still the two main levels; the cubicles on the second floor, and the 'wet area' on the ground floor. Everything has an air of decay, as if the management isn't sure whether they'll be open in six months; still, I met a delightful man..."

In the same issue of *Steam*, O'Hara published *MANSCOUNTRY: A Second Opinion* by Trent. "A lifetime membership is just $10. Lockers are $5 for twelve hours. Rooms are $15/8 hours. Monday nights, rooms are just $7.50. Wednesdays, rooms are $5/5 hours. A cubicle with a leather sling is the 'fantasy room.'...A lot of boys I know go to the baths. In Chicago, it's often too white and/or too old. One thing special about Manscountry is the age and racial mix. (Of the other two baths, one has decidedly less people of color, and the other is frequented by an older crowd.) It's reasonable prices and efforts at AIDS education and awareness make it special too. Sometimes called 'Dirty Old Manscountry,' a lot of its regulars are holdovers from the seventies when the place was new and they were fresh young things. It's nearly a shambles now, a mere shadow of its former glory, in an advanced state of disrepair. Sleazy is one thing, filth is another. Still, it appears that enough people still like the flavor of bathhouses and want to be informed about AIDS with the freedom to play safe…A long awaited refurbishing is rumored to be in the near future to clean up the place and make for more trick spaces. Once equipped with ballroom, orgy room, and snack bar, there were lots of places to trick inside the club, even without a room. Now, there's only the steam room or the open halls—and its rather unpleasant dealing with the leaky ceiling and the soggy carpeting, much less braving the swampy sauna. The Country Club, as it's also called, was one of the first to regularly leaflet and counsel on condom usage and STD testing. Weekend nights see a rush when the nearby bars close. The weeknights are the time to see the city people, especially Thursday night when Bistro Too hosts its popular Dollar Beer Night. Manscountry is the place to find all the children; young, old, black, white, Hispanic & Asian, athletes, students, cowboys, dancers & businessmen, half naked in hot pursuit of trade or just chillin'. To get there, come to Chicago and look for Bistro Too; it's right next door."

In "Through a Maze, Darkly," an essay from his collection *Rarely Pure and Never Simple* (Harrington Park Press, 1999), Scott O'Hara wrote once more about Man's Country. "The baths…that phrase conjures up so many images to me. The orgy room at Manscountry, all tactile and aural, no visuals, is one of the primal ones. The hot tub downstairs is another. Baths, in my humble opinion, should always have a hot tub. Without it, you may call them many things, but they aren't bathhouses. And that medieval grotto at Manscountry…! Dank and mildewed, condensation dripping from the ceiling, brick walls that looked like the original catacombs, with iron fixtures rusting away; who knows what bacterial menagerie lurked in the water? I loved it. Did I have sex in the hot tub? Undoubtedly—though the generally accepted practice was to catch someone's eye, then get out, spend an inordinate amount of time showering, and drying off, then saunter over to the steamroom (with a meaningful glance back at your potential partner). Once inside the steamroom…well, my modus operandi was to lie face down on the bench that bisected the room. If my quarry didn't find me, someone else soon did. It hardly mattered. At the baths, a dick is a dick is a dick."

Chapter Eleven

"I helped Chuck tear out the Bistro Too and build the Eagle," said Duke. "I was on the payroll, so I worked doing that as well as dancing. I cried like a baby when we tore out the spiral staircase and the big circular bar from Bistro Too. That bar started all this for me. But at the same time, we were tearing out something wonderful, we were building something that was going to be a leather hub."

When Bistro Too opened six years earlier, Chuck took the area beneath the main floor of Bistro Too and turned it into the Man's Country gym. Accessed through the bathhouse via the front desk, gym membership was included with a Man's Country membership. Proper gym attire was required. Working out was the cost of a locker. The gym was open daily from two in the afternoon until ten at night. Print ads of the period underlined an additional perk that members had by working out there. "The SEXsational Chicago Meatpackers are your personal weight trainers."

The Music Hall had been absorbed back into Man's Country, but the ground floor of Bistro Too was slated to be a part of this new bar, as was the level below it. The gym area closed, and that part of the bathhouse was revamped to become the lower level, or Pit, of Chuck's new leather bar, the Chicago Eagle. Chuck chose the name because, like leather itself, the eagle was a symbol for rough sex. The Chicago Eagle was not connected to any of the other gay leather Eagle bars located in other cities.

The entrance of the Chicago Eagle was in the alley through the cab of a semi. "I remember the traffic jam caused trying to get that thing in the alley," said Duke. "But it was also there to cover the zebra stripes on the wall from when the alley led to Bistro Too."

"Brilliant," added Rick Karlin. "I remember when they backed the semi in there. It was a brilliant move—brilliant marketing, brilliant decorating. That semi made the Eagle into something unique right away."

After entering the bed of the semi, patrons exited at the entrance of the bar. Above was a sign that read Home of International Mr. Leather in neon block letters. A doorman was at the door checking IDs. Inside the Eagle, porn played on several screens. The coat check was in a jail cell on the left. Down a narrow hallway were the bathrooms. A neon ejaculating penis denoted the men's room. Above the women's bathroom was a pair of neon boobs.

Inside the men's room was an elevated bootblack chair. "On one wall in the men's room were the floor plans of the original Gold Coast in a mounted frame," said Jon Krongaard. "Above the urinals was a mounted photo of my partner, Ken, and I kissing. Terry Gaskins had taken the photo for a Stop AIDS Chicago poster. So, our friends used to say, 'I'm going to the men's room to see Ken and Jon.'"

A large island bar dominated the front room on the ground level of the Eagle. The main floor also featured a pool table and a few high boys. On the walls were strips of corrugated metal, giving the place a hard, industrial feel. The Chicago Eagle also became a repository with an abundance of iconic leather memorabilia on display—posters, erotic art, and as with Chuck's other businesses, the enormous murals of Etienne.

The lower level at the Chicago Eagle, known as the Pit or the Grease Pit, was a hotspot for adventurous leatherfolk. Ron Ehemann explained the fanfare that accompanied every Pit opening, "There was a huge trap door on the floor and a chain going up to a block and tackle pulley. At eleven o'clock, they would open the door—the pulley and chain made a loud noise like something out of a *Frankenstein* movie when the door was being opened."

"The sign for the Pit was the same one that was in the Gold Coast when it was at 501 North Clark," added Dan Neniskis. "The sign was a neon arrow pointing down and inside the arrow in vertical lettering, it said, The Pit. The entrance was a trap door, so it was just an opening on the floor, so it had a chain link fence around the opening to make sure no one fell in the hole."

Admittance to the hardcore downstairs area required a major article of leather, latex, or a uniform. The rule was strictly enforced. Descending into the Pit, there was an enormous hand-carved serpentine bar along the back wall. To the right was a mannequin in a cage with real bars, a bootblack chair, and a St. Andrew's Cross that saw plenty of activity.

"In the Pit there were cages built into the wall," recalled Dan Atwell, "with real bars. Inside were mannequins in leather. One was a flogging scene. The Eagle was big on atmosphere. The enormous Etienne paintings did that—this scene did too. Creating the right mood was a big part of that bar, especially in the Pit. I remember there was also a huge safe down there that was five feet high and had to have weighed ten tons."

"After we finished building the Eagle," added Duke. "I started bartending there as well. We were so fucking busy. I worked mostly upstairs, but sometimes downstairs too. Down there was Harry Shattuck's spot. He was an icon, and he had his following. You could always tell when Harry was working because his regulars were lining the bar. There was one guy who used to order a bourbon and tipped $100 if Harry stirred the ice with his dick."

In *Leatherman,* Harry Shattuck explained his connection to the Pit at the Chicago Eagle. "I made those padded benches with eyeholes that were sort of like sawhorses. I had about 4-6 of them...I brought those with me to the Grease Pit at the Eagle. I disinfected that basement. No one wanted to be down there because it stunk, but I cleaned it out and then all the bartenders wanted to be down there, but I was like, 'No, this is mine.' I made the St. Andrew's Cross that was down there as well."

RV became a regular Eagle patron shortly after it opened. "I always had a good time. It was nice and friendly. No one was a sloppy drunk there. People at the Eagle seemed less standoffish, more down to earth. I met Harry Shattuck. He was so kind. I told him I was a photographer and he encouraged me. He modeled for me. He introduced me to people. Harry and Chuck really helped my career. Through them I met so many people. I got a reputation for being respectful of the kink world and what people are into—and I became a fetish photographer."

There was no shortage of fetish at the Eagle. There was even a Fetish Night as well as Uniform Night, Movie and Pizza night, and Lesbian Night. "I bartended in the Pit on Wednesdays for a few months," said

Vicki Joholski-Grooms. "For Lesbian Night, Chuck dressed me in leather to the nines. There really was nothing like dressing that way and going down those stairs. It felt sexy as hell. On Lesbian Night the women came to play pool and get nasty. There were plenty of dark corners in the Pit for getting nasty. It was always a good time, but Lesbian Night didn't go over. The Eagle was an established gay male leather place and the Pit was like the crown jewel. Chuck wanted women at the bar, but he was a little ahead of his time on wanting that mix. Lesbian Night ended in under a year."

In an effort to boost business on the slowest night of the week, Tuesday night became Leather Night at the Chicago Eagle. The plan worked. Tuesdays became a huge night there. On Leather Night there were raffles for leather gear, fifty-cent draft beers, and plenty of leatherfolk eager to play. Something else that brought in the crowds on Leather Night was that the down-and-dirty Pit at the Eagle was open.

"The Eagle was like a mini Gold Coast," said Dean Ogren. "It was very reminiscent of the old days. I loved going there. Chuck would often be there. It was nice to just sit there and have a drink and a relaxed chat with him." Ogren also liked having the bar in the center of the room. "There is nothing better for cruising than an island bar. There was excitement in that in moving around, in seeing someone across the bar, in the chase—where you eye someone and think, I've got to have some of that, and then the game and the dance of trying to get it."

"The main bar itself at the Eagle was very cool," recalled Dan Neniskis. "They took a bunch of coins and paper money as well as different Gold Coast newspaper ads and scattered them across the bar and then went over it with some sort of coating, so they were sealed on the bar."

"After my first great love passed, I kind of retired my leathers," shared Robert Kimmons. "At first I was resistant to go to the Eagle, but when I did, I felt comfortable. I didn't feel judged like I did when I went to bars on Halsted. It didn't matter if I was ten pounds overweight or whatever. The Eagle was a big part of my recovery. I gained self-acceptance there. I was wary of people, but the Eagle allowed me to put myself out there and see where I fit in. I remember being in the Pit during IML weekend. It was packed, wall-to-wall people, but I felt so connected to the community of leathermen in that space. I learned and experienced a lot at the Eagle about being a leatherman and about BDSM."

The Eagle served as a meeting spot for various leather clubs, groups, and organizations. *Gay Chicago* photographer Terry Gaskins began covering events there in the early 1990s. "I was at the Eagle almost every week. Sometimes I went to the Pit. Mostly I went there to photograph titleholders—all the leather misters and bootblacks, any sort of leather contest." Gaskins continued. "One time at the Eagle there was a slave auction. I don't know who nominated me, but I wound up being on the auction block. I ended up getting the highest bid. Chuck bid on me to help raise money for whatever it was. He just wanted to donate the money. He never cashed in his bid on me or anything."

"I started working part time at the Eagle in 1993," said Robert Harvey. "That quickly turned into fulltime. When I got the job, I was already a regular. I liked the Eagle, I felt like it was trying to become what Touche had been on Lincoln had been with things like whipping demos and the action in the Pit. The Eagle drew old guard leather people. They had a code of how SM works and had a great amount of integrity about that. At the Eagle, the guys who were in the bike clubs were really into bikes—that kind of thing."

Harvey added, "For the most part, I bartended in the Pit with Harry Shattuck who liked to crack his whip a half inch from me. He was so precise with that thing. The Pit was dim anyway, but at some point a light bulb would get unscrewed. There was some light from the pinball machine. Sunday nights were my big night for tips. The rest of the weekend it was mostly tourists. About two in the morning on Sundays all the service industry people would roll in with cash from the weekend—lots of shots. And from two to four in the morning, I made a fortune."

The Pit at the Chicago Eagle was also popular because it had a very busy bathroom. "The bathroom downstairs wasn't big," recalled Harvey, "But when we closed so many people would come out of there. It was wild. They just kept coming. Sometimes there were at least thirty people crammed in there. When you turned on the light there were popper bottles and everything else on that floor. I was just happy I didn't have to clean."

"When you approached that bathroom, you could feel heat coming from the entrance," laughed Wayne Hussey. "My favorite thing to do in the Pit was to sit and have a drink and talk with other regulars or watch the dynamics at play. The stairs to the Pit were treacherous in boots. There was no railing. I remember watching the Pit virgins come down those stairs with their eyes wide."

Hussey also did some demos at the Eagle. "Fire play, flogging, and impact play. People were given an education in other ways as well—like how to be in a scene but not be seen—that you are a spectator unless you are invited to participate. There were other things too, about how to be respectful in the BDSM world. It taught how to be clear about stating your boundaries. For me, the Pit was about exploring boundaries, and sometimes it was about pushing them."

"I discovered the Eagle around 1995," said James Lahiff. "The first time I went there, I was hanging out with friends, and no one wanted to go with me to a leather bar. So I put on my leather pants and engineer boots, my vest—and rode my ten-speed there from Ukrainian Village to the Eagle in July. I was a sweaty mess by the time I got there. Someone I knew was working the door and said, 'Get your ass in here.' I liked the place right away. It was quiet and I remember I thought it would be busier. All I had to do was wait a couple hours. By midnight there were a hundred leather guys there."

After IML 1998, the Eagle underwent a drastic remodeling. Behind the main bar, the wood had started to rot. As a solution to the decay, a concrete floor was poured. The Pit was then closed and a back bar, aka the Clubroom, opened. Two doorways on either side of the main room led to the Clubroom. Inside was a pinball machine. Against the wall and above the bar, two monitors played porn. After the renovation and the closing of the Pit, the dark bathroom/playroom off the Clubroom became the new spot for action.

Dan Atwell, who started bartending at the Chicago Eagle following the August 1998 renovation, recalled the Clubhouse bathroom. "The room was very dark, but your eyes adjust. I used to go in there looking for glasses. There were three places they could be—on the windowsill, in the trough, or in the sink. I can still hear Jim Stiveirs yelling out in that back area, 'If I can hear it, smell it, or see it—you're doing it wrong.'"

Atwell enjoyed working at the Eagle. "People were friendly, more accepting of each other's kinks and fetishes, and just less pretentious than a lot of bars. If you were there and dressed like you belonged there, there was a tacit understanding that you were one of us."

"In the main room, the ceiling was so high that you couldn't even reach it on a ladder," recalled Atwell. "That front area at the Eagle was a huge box—but those giant Etienne murals were fantastic. It was a nice benefit of the job to stare at those all night. One was a master with the slave in a collar at his feet and another mural was of two guys standing at a bar with their dicks out. The back area had some Etienne artwork as well. All the art in the Pit went straight to the Leather Archives when the downstairs closed."

Atwell worked the closing shift at the Eagle four nights a week for a decade. He said that the Eagle bartenders didn't have a dress code. "The fact that we would be in leather was just a given. We did have a list of rules. I remember one was that we were told to address everyone as Sir. People knew the nights I worked. Three of those nights I chose the music. Mondays I played classic rock and roll, Wednesdays I played punk, and on Thursdays I played dance music, but dark masculine industrial dance music. Our sound booth, which was really a closet, was on the right as you came into the bar. When I first started, we were using a five carousel CD player, but eventually we hooked up our IPods, which was much better."

Atwell described the layout of the main room. "As you came into the Eagle, there was the sound booth. Next was a St. Andrew's cross, but it was different than the one in the Pit. Then came a pool table and then a barber's chair. A bootblack chair had been there, but the barber's chair replaced it—and we had Barber Night. I remember that because I was duct-taped to that chair and had my head shaved."

Jon Kronrgaard recalled another change with the remodeling. "No more dancers on weekends in the front bar. Before the change, there was a cage to the left coming in the door. If you came in on the weekend, there was usually a young gay guy in a jockstrap dancing there."

Atwell added that for the holidays, employees received a bonus with their Christmas card. "The job was good money and great tips. We were open 364 days a year. We closed on Christmas Eve because Chuck said people should be with friends and family. He closed Man's Country on Christmas Eve too. I owe Chuck and the Renslow Family a lot. They paid for me to go to rehab, and then held my job for me. That says a lot right there."

"The Eagle was a lot of fun," said Dave Plomin. "The atmosphere was a turn on, like a fantasy with the murals, the dark atmosphere, the stale beer and smoke smell, the macho crowd, and that popular backroom..."

"That back bar area also had some set pieces from IML," said Jon Krongaard. "There was the painted brick wall back there, some Dom panels, and different set pieces." The backroom also featured a motorcycle chained to the floor.

"I was living in Ravenswood," said AH. "The Eagle was a little scary, but I was curious. When I eventually went, I felt like I had discovered this cool universe that I did not even know existed. Being a naïve twink, I had no idea. This was where I felt I belonged. The backroom there was hit or miss. At times there was this spontaneous eroticism and connection with all these hot men, and other times it was off. Part of the excitement was in not knowing what it would be."

AH continued, "I was in a long-distance relationship and when my lover was in town, we went to the Eagle together. We both ended up in the backroom getting done by two different people. It was so hot sharing this erotic experience. We were each having sex with different people, but we were connected by this eye contact in the darkness. It was the hottest thing to share those euphoric moments with him, but not together."

"I went there from probably 1995 to 2000," said Rick Parker. "I liked to go there and play pool and pinball. The Eagle was quieter. I wasn't necessarily a leather guy, but I felt more comfortable. I met a very good friend of mine, Jim Stiveir, who was a bartender there. He was a wonderful mentor for me and showed me so many things. Jim was hyperglycemic, so he had to keep something to eat behind the bar. I remember, he loved to show off and deep throat his banana before he took a bite."

"I loved the Eagle," said Adam A. "It was a great union of friendly neighborhood bar with a sexy vibe. It had no attitude and no line to get in. I wasn't a muscle queen or anything like that. I was comfortable there.

I became pretty much a regular. Guys were friendly. The bartenders were friendly. Once at that back bar, I was talking to an older gentleman. It was always easy to talk to people there. Anyway, so this guy I am talking to whips out the biggest cock I had ever seen, and I just dropped to my knees and went to town on it for a least a half hour."

"Sometimes some of my coworkers and I would go there for a drink," recalled Marino. "I knew the bartenders. Once when I was there having a drink, a guy offered me two hundred dollars to fill his glass with pee, but I just went to the bathroom. I told him I wished he had asked ten minutes ago."

"Once in the Clubroom we hung all these long pieces of fabric," recalled Duke. "We just stapled them to the ceiling with a staple gun. We did a lot of them, so all this cloth was hung down to make this dark maze. I think the whole reason was that we can't tell anyone to stop doing something that we can't see them doing."

James Lahiff recalled the Clubhouse bathroom. "It was like some 1970s gay sex fantasy where HIV didn't exist. I didn't do anything there. I was a big proponent of wrap it up [wear a condom] so I was not really part of that. I could not get over the pure carnality of it all. What kept me coming was the sense of bar community—a different community that wore leather and came out at night. We became a kind of family"

Lahiff continued, "I was at the Eagle one night in 2001 and there was a leather contest. I was wearing my leathers and had shaved my head the day before. I was there to checkout guys. When they asked the contestants to line up, my name was called. The bartenders had signed me up. I ended up winning. I was Mr. September in the 2002 Men of Male Hide Leathers Calendar, which was done for charity. The prize was a gift voucher to Male Hide which I used for a nice leather vest."

"The Eagle attracted a different type than the leather bars on Halsted Street, which were more about fashion," said PG. "I wasn't into leather really, but I loved the historical weight of the leather community. That was the allure for me. Men talked to me there, but I wasn't looking for friendships necessarily, I was looking for dick. To the men I chatted with I was just a curious young gay guy—that was the role that was assigned me, and I gladly accepted that role."

AH added, "When the Eagle closed, it felt like we were losing a part of our world, and it was not coming back. It was saying goodbye to this place where we could explore and be free. The Eagle was a place to be uninhibited, but at the same time learn the unspoken gay code of ethics. To see it close was heartbreaking."

In a *Leatherman* interview, Chuck spoke about the Chicago Eagle. "It was the wrong location, the wrong time. It didn't have that mystique that the old Gold Coast had. There was an aura in the old Gold Coast that you felt...When all was said and done it [the Chicago Eagle] was just another leather bar. It was popular and it did well, but the magic, the ambience was off. It never quite made it—not good, not bad—but not special either—just another leather bar."

When the Chicago Eagle closed in 2006, Man's Country again reclaimed the newly available space. Once more the building was restructured. The area was converted into more rooms for the bathhouse. With the extra room at Man's Country, Chuck also installed a remodeled art walk, a fetish area for exhibitionists and voyeurs, and a glory hole area.

Chuck Renslow and Ron Ehemann at White Party outside Bistro Too

Bistro Too grand opening invitation. Courtesy Ron Ehemann.

Memory Lane autographed photo, courtesy of Ron Ehemann.

Gay Chicago *newspaper ad for Divine's appearance at Bistro Too.*

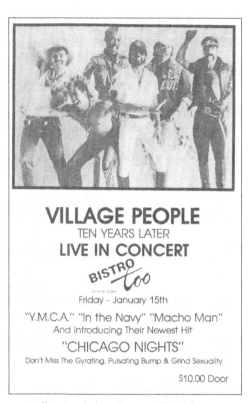

Village People flier. Courtesy of Ron Ehemann.

The Meatpackers. Photo courtesy of Ron Ehemann.

The entrance to the Chicago Eagle was through the bed of a semi. Photo: Ron Ehemann

Chicago Eagle Staff. Photo: Ron Ehemann.

Motorcycles parked outside the Chicago Eagle. Photo: Ron

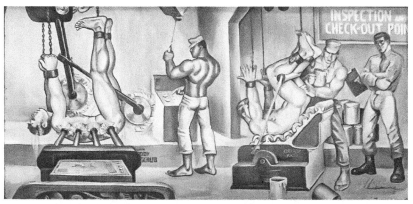

Detail of the Etienne mural, Car Wash, which hung outside the shower area at Man's Country. Courtesy Leather Archives and Museum

Sarabia & Maria. Photo : St Sukie de la Croix.

The main staircase at Man's Country. Photo: @victorinox67

Dedication of the Chuck Renslow street sign. Photo courtesy of Tracy Baim, Windy City Times

Chuck Renslow street sign. Author's collection.

Chapter Twelve

"The first time I went to Man's Country was in 1983," said Robert Kimmons. "This was a different crowd than the one that went to the Unicorn. This crowd was more mature, more diverse—not the Halsted Street crowd. Going there I got to experience a wider variety of men. I felt comfortable. There was no pressure. Man's Country felt more relaxed. I never got a room. I liked walking around. I felt comfortable there, but I wouldn't walk around barefoot. I wore shoes when I went there. My favorite part was the grotto. My favorite memories of Man's Country took place there."

"After my first time in 1988," said Ward B. "I then went once every few months for a couple years. If you were gay in Chicago, Man's Country was a rite of passage. It was for me anyway. If you wanted to get off, it was Man's Country or Little Jim's. Man's Country wasn't a dating place. I just went there to trick—but I met a couple of people there that I'm still friends with today. I usually got a locker. I liked to cruise the halls. The wildest place was always the wet area. It was so decadent. The area had a dirty gym kind of smell. I liked that. That area got so wild that half the fun was watching."

"I went there for the first time around 1990," said James Lahiff. "I was so nervous. I felt so out of place. I was this super-skinny, fluffy-haired blonde in an oversized New Order T-shirt and baggie shorts. Going in there, I loved the mix of men. You could smell sex in the air. I thought I found heaven. The guys at Man's Country were not like the guys in the boy bars—they were men."

"Man's Country played to a broad spectrum," said Dean Ogren. "In its heyday, that grotto and whirlpool was a whole fantasy area, with the waterfall and the area behind the waterfall. The sexuality around the whirlpool and all that was very open, very easy, and very casual. That area always reminded me of a gay Playboy Mansion."

Derek Spenser returned to Man's Country after years of having been away. "The biggest difference was that there was hardly anyone there. Even though it was rundown, it still felt special, comfortable. The place was iconic—the light fixtures, the murals."

"Sometimes after the Eagle closed, we would continue the party at Man's Country," recalled Rick Parker. "I would go there with my friend Jim and some others from the closing Eagle crowd. I liked that it was sort of seedy and dark. I remember platform seating in the room [Music Hall] upstairs and porn playing on the big screen. I liked the downstairs more. I liked being down there and meeting people in the showers and hot tub."

"Vicki, who was working as Chuck's secretary at the time, and I, used to take our morning breaks together," said Jon Krongaard. "I was working at the IML office in the anteroom of Chuck's office, so Vicki and I would have coffee and a cigarette in the lobby by the fish tank. Guys would come down from the Music Hall in their towels, see a woman in the bathhouse, do a one-eighty, and zoom back up the stairs. That used to crack us up. Sometimes regulars hung around and chatted. I met so many interesting people at Man's Country. Guys from all walks of life."

"I think I was the first woman to work there," said Vicki Joholski-Grooms. "As Chuck's secretary, I hung out there quite a bit, and took my breaks in the lobby or talking at the front desk. Guys used to be a little surprised to see me, but it got to feel like home. When I think of my time at Man's Country it always brings a smile to my face."

Grooms, who became a Renslow Family member, shared the bathhouse's importance during the holidays. "Christmas Eve was a special day for the Family. On that day the Family were the only ones in Man's Country, and we all got to enjoy all the benefits it had to offer."

"Man's Country felt special," said Jeremy G. "It was a place of sexual magic. I always got a room even though I never brought guys back to it. I got off on sex in the common areas. I liked those platforms in the Music Hall. My room was where I regrouped and took a break from the sexual energy. Then, when I was ready, I went out and threw myself into it again. I liked getting my money's worth."

"I was terrified to go for years," said David C. "My self-esteem was that bad. The first couple times I went, I passed out there. It was not pretty. Later, I went to Man's Country sober. Once I got past the smell, I had some good times. It was a sexual awakening. I never understood the socializing. The guys who ate breakfast and gossiped down at the snack bar mystified me—that was not me at all."

Brian Kirst was nervous when he applied for a job at Man's Country. After filling out the application, Kirst was given a tour. "I was told this was where guest porn stars and strippers performed every Friday and Saturday. After being informed of what my duties would entail, I was told to think about it and call back if interested." Kirst accepted the job and, for couple of months in 1997, he worked at the snack shop in the lobby outside the Music Hall. "The special when I worked was a $1.99 for hot dog and chips. I sold a lot of them, but the two months I was there I only took in my salary once. In other words, the Snack Shop didn't pay for itself, but Chuck liked to have it as a place for the members to relax. A regular movie played in that room nonstop as well. So during my ten at night to six in the morning shifts, I would see the movie four or five times. *The Bodyguard* and *Bird on a Wire* were two movies I saw a lot."

One member recalled sitting in the snack bar, pretending to watch *Caddyshack*. "But I was really cruising and keeping an eye on the guys going in and out of the Music Hall."

Kirst added, "Some nights groups of like-minded men would gather near me and play cards by the snack bar and watch the films playing in the lounge and gossip about their daily activities. I would look forward to seeing them every weekend."

"One Saturday morning," added Kirst, "Chuck partitioned off a couple of areas for a leather event for all sexes. I came in to work the snack shop for the attendees. Most of the participants were gay men, but there were a number of straight couples thrown into the mix, as well."

Kirst wrote about one of the women he met that day in his one-man show about working at the bathhouse, *Undercover in the House of Love*. "She's giving me 'mom in the neighborhood' energy...calling me honey, tipping me a buck or two every time she orders a coffee or a soda from me. I wonder if she knows that only two feet away from where she's standing, I saw an out of towner start to give a regular a blowjob last night. The manager, of course, quickly shushed them away into the ball room area where that activity is allowed. No free form sexual riots in open spaces on his watch! Come to think of it, she probably wouldn't care. She's now happily recounting to her girlfriend about the spanking party that she and her husband and an acquaintance held the weekend before. "I was supposed to count every other slap, but I forgot and was counting every single one!" she giggles happily. "After a few minutes, Dennis discovered what was happening...and, oh my goodness, we had to stop right then and there and start the paddling all over again! I was so red and sore when we were done!!" Although good natured exasperation colors her voice, I can tell she really wasn't disappointed about that particular turn of events in the least."

A quarter century after his stint working there, Kirst shared his most enduring memory of Man's Country. "The sense of nurturing and community. Leather folks would stop and explain their activities and kinks to me with passion. I learned about fisting and sounding and began to understand that if an activity involved enjoyment and consent, there was little that was weird or incomprehensible about it."

Photographer Terry Gaskins recalled her frequent gigs at Man's Country. "In the early 1990s, I was the only woman in there. At *Gay Chicago* part of my job was covering events. The first time I went I had no idea what to do. I stood in line and the clerk asked if I wanted a towel and a locker. I said I was there to take pictures. He buzzed me in. I was terrified to see guys I knew, so I went down and waited for Chuck in the snack bar while staring at the wall. Chuck found me and asked if I wanted something to drink or a hot dog or a cinnamon roll. I said I was good. Then he showed me the Music Hall. The whole time we were walking to get there I tried to look at the ceiling. Chuck said if I ever needed to use the Music Hall for photos or anything, I was free to use it and that I was always welcome in any of his establishments. So I waited at the dressing room to photograph this dancer, and the guy came out with a complete erection. I had to wait after the show to photograph him. In the meantime, I just stood there and stared at the dressing room door."

Gaskins continued, "We eventually had a system down where I entered through the Eagle and go up straight up to the Music Hall that way. Sometimes I spent the show in the control booth with Ron who usually did the lights and sound. After I would go down and photograph the guy, or he would come upstairs, or I would photograph them outside the Music Hall. I photographed lots of porn stars—Caesar, Sonny Markham, Jeff Stryker, a lot. I saw some crazy things. Once around Pride there was a real tiger upstairs roaming around the lobby by the Music Hall. I think he was part of an act. I remember the tiger because, well, it's the only time I ever photographed a tiger in a gay bathhouse." Several members and staff also recalled the tiger. Apparently, after being in the bathhouse, the tiger then spent a good portion of the evening at the Eagle.

"I started going in 1992 and probably went every week until I left town in 1996," said Mauricio. "I was entering the gay community in my thirties. Man's Country was where I went to figure myself out. Man's Country was kind of grimy and stark. The carpet was bad, but the people were interesting and more earnest. It was less racially separated, definitely. There was every type of person there. Going there was identity affirming for me. I felt comfortable, appreciated, and welcome. It was a big playground that had everything."

Mauricio continued, "One of the first times I went there I ran into a gentleman carrying a suitcase. I went to his room and he had all sorts of SM outfit gear, paraphernalia, and toys. I was fascinated and explored fashion that day. I dressed up in four different costume variations with collars, chaps, jockstrap, boots, mask, and cuffs and then he paraded me around the club by a chain. That day I discovered the importance of sexual apparel and some things about control and submission. Man's Country was like an advent calendar that way—you never knew what was behind a door."

"Man's Country was wrong in all the right ways," recalled Mitchell Fain. "I liked that it was seedy and smelled like sweat and cum. There was something primal there. It was a thrilling throwback to more exciting days. This is what being a sexual outlaw felt like. I liked feeling that I was doing something really subversive. By going there, I pushed my boundaries sexually. I'm smaller, so I also worried about being adventurous sexually while still being physically safe. Man's Country was a way for me to explore my deviant fantasies and feel protected. If things went wrong, I could yell out, or leave. I learned how to cruise at Man's

Country and learned about handling rejection there. In some ways it felt like I was taught to be gay there. It was a safe place for people to explore themselves. That also meant that if you went there and you decided that you never wanted to go there again—you still learned something about yourself in the process."

David Weeks discovered Man's Country soon after moving to Chicago in 1996. "I was newly out and what drew me was the images I had seen in posters and fliers. I liked it dim, seedy, and dark. Man's Country fit my expectations of what a bathhouse should be, and that made it very hot. I went on off-nights because they were less intense. The place had this history. So as our gay world got more mainstreamed around then, Man's Country felt like a little part of this secret history that wasn't ours anymore. I liked the Music Hall. They had this two-leveled carpeted seating around the perimeter that was conducive to group activity."

Phillip Bernal liked watching everyone get their freak on. "It was a blast being in this world with all these amazing naked men. There was the size of the place and the art—some of the art was very valuable. My favorite part was the grotto area. Warm water and I'm in heaven. There is something very communal and inviting about sharing a body of water. And it's an easy way to connect. Your leg can slide over if they respond you're there, if they ease their foot away, it's a soft rejection."

"I went to Man's Country with friends," said Malone Sizelove. "We would hang out for hours. We would talk and each of us might go hook up. Then we would get back together and gossip about who was there and who was hot. There were usually some fresh faces. They also had live DJs on the weekend and I know they paid well. I remember when I went there, I would think that even if I didn't get laid, at least I would hear some good music."

St Sukie de la Croix photographed a kink carnival at Man's Country for *Nightspots*. "The one I attended had a very burlesque feel. There was a woman fire-eater. Lots of women were there in general. During the event, Chuck walked up to me and said, 'I've spent years trying to get women here, and here they are.' I remember that night I took a photo of Teri Yaki standing at the urinal in Man's Country and another drag queen pretending to drink the piss." Working for the paper, Sukie returned a couple times to photograph the strippers. "Both times they came out buck-naked. This was for *Nightspots*—our motto was, 'no holes, no poles.' I waited until the end of the act and then took them to the DJ booth."

RV also photographed the dancers and the visiting porn stars. "I did that for a couple of years. I would shoot them from the DJ booth while they were performing and then I would sometimes do studio time with them as well. We would do that during the daytime. We would close up the Music Hall and I would set up using a studio background."

As a Chicago native, PG was aware of Man's Country long before he first went there in 2000. "I had always thought of it as kind of gross and I wasn't far off—the upholstery was ripped, the carpet was worn, and even the elastic band on the keychain didn't have any elasticity. Then I went and hooked up with this guy who actually looked like a 1970s fantasy, a very hot guy with the handlebar moustache and all, so it kind of made sense."

Ian L. went to Man's Country for a couple years from 2002 through 2004. "I had been sober for years and then at IML 25, I went to Man's Country after. The doors were open between the Eagle and the bathhouse. I was in superhero rubber and followed a couple of guys into their room and they were shooting up and that was the first time I stuck a needle in my arm. I'm sober now, but that was in the depths of my addiction. I would walk around [Man's Country] and see it was pretty shabby—but I liked how it felt gritty. I wasn't a part of the history there. I came too late for that, but I appreciated it. In my addiction, Man's Country was a place for me to hide out. If it was Monday morning and I was in no shape for work, Man's Country was where I went. There were a few of us there. We could go there and not be judged. If I was too jacked up or sketched out to work, I didn't want to be home. Man's Country was a place to come down. I didn't want to know if it was day or night. Time was suspended there. A lot of us went to Man's Country to sleep. It was a place of sadness—addiction is not pretty. But it felt safe coming down there. It was a place to hide out when there seemed no place else to go. Maybe being there kept me alive."

"I'm HIV positive," shared a member. "And I look HIV positive. My body changed. I don't look like a negative person. I'm not always welcome [at bathhouses] because of that. But I think more men like me went to Man's Country because we didn't feel ostracized there."

"I was working at the IML office when they gutted the north end of Man's Country to build Full Kit Leather," said Jon Krongaard. "I remember going over to look at the progress. The whole area was stripped. No rooms. They ripped out walls, the floor was stripped down, another wall was peeled down to this green and off-white Grecian wallpaper. I asked the kid working there if he found anything interesting and he said he found two gold chains and a set of false teeth. Later I mentioned the conversation to Joey [McDonald], who worked with me at the IML office. Then he said, 'Oh I know whose those are. When I worked here there was a guy who always came in and sometimes when he checked out, he would say, 'Well, I lost another pair of false teeth.'"

"I came here from Italy," said Marino. "Three days after my plane landed in Chicago I was working at Man's Country. I began working there in April of 1999 and was there for eighteen years. I started as an attendant, and then I was a clerk at the front desk, then I became assistant manager, and then I became the manager. I mostly ran the place for the last four or five years. I did my best to keep it going. Towards the end it was impossible to repair especially with business down."

Marino continued, "When I first arrived, I never imagined a place like this existed. Everyone was so nice. My English was so bad, but everyone, the members too, tried to help me and teach me stuff. There were many memories with customers, mostly good people—a lot of great guys. I made friends with customers and coworkers. I adapted very quickly. I didn't mingle with the members for probably the first year. Then I had a lot of fun, but I stopped again after I became assistant manager or manager because I would get asked work questions."

"You had to be prepared for anything," added Marino. "I had a guy pull a gun on me. Once there was a fight upstairs and when I ran up there one of the guys pulled a knife on me. The police ended up handling both situations. We had a great crew, people stayed at their jobs, and everyone worked better because they got to understand one another. The hardest part of the job was firing people. I fired very few people. I did not want to be responsible for putting someone out on the street. I told people when they worked there, I expected them to apply themselves and if the job isn't for them, to do something different."

Marino continued, "Chuck and Ron treated me like family. If I need to call someone, it's still Ron. I had not even been working there three years when Chuck gave me the key to his house. He knew I didn't have people here. He said I was free to come over for dinner or just come be with people. They treated me like a family member. I'm in California now. I miss Man's Country. I started there when I was thirty and it was the next eighteen years of my life. I miss the family, my coworkers, and the customers—even the ones that were sometimes a pain in the ass."

Spike worked there for two or three years starting in 2007. "Things weren't good, my lover died, I had nothing, and I moved back to Chicago. Chuck always told me if I needed help to ask, so he gave me a job at Man's Country. I cleaned, did laundry, and made up the rooms for special occasions. When we did that, we put two little wine bottles on the end of the bed and mints on the pillow."

Spike added that sometimes work was a lot of fun. "One of my first nights there was New Year's Eve, Gary B. and I put poppers in the air vent to get everyone fucked up. In ten minutes, the place smelled like poppers, and it lasted for five hours. We got in trouble. Chuck called us in and said, 'You can't do that.'"

Spike also lived at Man's Country for a while. "They let you do that if you were down on your luck—a few of us lived there. We weren't squatters, we came in and checked out, but we lived there. The Family took care of people. I was never tardy checking out or late for work. When I lived there, I didn't wear a towel, I wore mostly sweats. I treated it like it was my room even though the room changed every time. At the end of my shift, I just went down to the guy at the front desk and asked for a room. It was never an issue. I was grateful to have a place. Two people died when I was working there, but that place was part of saving my life."

"One of the first times I went there," said Victorinox67, "I ran into Chuck and followed him to his office. He had a big desk with an arsenal of whips, paddles, and dildos. He gave me a really hard spanking." Soon after, he started working there. "I heard Chuck spanking different young men in his office while I worked there. I could tell when I saw them come out of his office. It showed on their faces that they got one of his spankings. Chuck's spankings were rough."

Victorinox67 worked as the assistant engineer of Man's Country from 2006-2010. "I did general maintenance mostly—painting, repairing, changing lights, some electrical, construction, and remodeling the rooms. Plumbing was always a problem as well, leaks in the sauna. It eventually was closed more than it was open. I needed work so I always showed up and was willing to do whatever needed to be done. I was grateful, but the building needed deep work. Things were always breaking down."

"I met so many people there," Victorinox67 continued, "A couple men lived there. They got up, got ready for work, and came back, checked in...and then went off to work the next day. The worst part about working there were the drugs. People locking themselves in their rooms or passing out with the door locked. Many people were taken out of that place in an ambulance wearing nothing but a towel."

In a 2010 interview with Alex Godfrey for *Vice*, Chuck addressed the upkeep of Man's Country, including the odor. "We've had the health department investigate us and we are clean, I've got two cleanup people, this place is spotless—the problem is, it's old. And a lot of people equate it to these new bathhouses, and yeah: we look tacky by comparison. But we are clean. We just put new carpet in the whole place. Our competitors on the other hand don't even have carpeting, they've got tiled floors. We're 35 years old. But it's not a question of whether we're dirty or anything. As far as odor, there's odor in every damned bathhouse you go to..."

"Chuck told me he did not want Man's Country to be like the Unicorn," said Sarabia, referring to the North Halsted St. bathhouse where Steamworks is today. "Chuck said, we're not the front of the street, we're the back alley. Man's Country was down and dirty, raunchy, a little terrifying, and very sexy."

"My boyfriend at the time and I sometimes got a room," said Wayne Hussey, "But we would have to be in piggy mode to overlook the condition of the place. For us, Man's Country was a place to let loose and not have to play by any rules. It was a chance to be together in a new environment and it was also a chance for us to explore, both together and apart."

"Most of the drug use I saw was downstairs," said Shane K. "It had a different feel down there. There was no music playing, so it was quiet, which made it eerie to hear moaning or whispering or whatever because it was hard to tell exactly where it was coming from."

"I didn't mind the ceiling leaks or anything like that. It was thrilling. There was history there. I felt comfortable there. It was more relaxed about body expectations," said Ziggy Leroy, "There wasn't the Boystown aesthetic. For a while there was two-level seating in the Music Hall and then there were church pews around the outside. Things were interesting there. I enjoyed staying most of my time and taking in the atmosphere, like those murals on the stairway to the Music Hall. It didn't need to be that opulent, but it was. I appreciated that. People were nicer here, they hung out. When you passed them in the halls people were more likely to stop and talk. I have had some deep conversations with people I have met there, but even without talking there was a feeling of understanding each other—a kinship, I suppose. We may have nothing in common, but we have something in common. That's why we're here."

Israel Wright recalled the Music Hall. "There were pews along one side and then gray carpeted risers on the other side. They had porn playing on the screen, and in the area underneath the DJ booth I recall some foam wedge padding. I also remember one of those circular couches in the middle of the dance floor beneath the disco ball for a while."

"I liked going to the Music Hall during the day," said David Rustile. "I enjoyed just going there and sitting. There would be some weird disco soundtrack playing from years ago. It was a good place to chill and be alone sometimes too."

"The music was amazing," said Shane K. "The first time I went there this European electronic synth pop was playing, but they were these really dark remixes I had never heard before. I loved it. The music was ideal for the environment. Other times I would hear 1970s disco, which had a haunted quality in the Music Hall—it was so dark in there with that one mirror ball and no one ever dancing. But once in the Music Hall they were playing Barry White and this beefy guy was in the middle of the dance floor doing cartwheels and all these gymnastics while wearing a towel. I stood there and waited for the towel to fall off, but it never did. He knew I was watching him, but he didn't react. He did his routine for the duration of the Barry White song."

"People can meet on the Internet now," said Chuck in 2010. "A lot of gay bars are going down, there used to be a dozen leather bars in Chicago, now there are only two. And the one thing that's really saving bathhouses is that if someone meets someone on the Internet and they don't want to go to each other's house, they can meet here. It's neutral ground. But things have changed, yeah. More people cruise on the Internet now than anywhere else." (Alex Godfrey, "Man's Country: A Man's a Club for Men," *Vice*, 2010).

"I worked the check in at Man's Country from 2007 to 2014," said Robert Harvey. "When I started, there were still lines on the weekend, but over the time I was there, the business just fizzled away. A lot of that job was babysitting. I called ambulances pretty regularly. GHB and crystal were the main culprits. Chuck even took one guy out of the lobby of Man's Country straight to rehab. Chuck hated crystal. One time I had to call an ambulance, because this guy who was a regular was obviously having a drug seizure. The paramedics said I probably saved his life. From that point on, I was dead to him because I called an ambulance. Sometimes no good deed went unpunished there. People would come in and they would be too drunk. I wouldn't let them in. They couldn't even walk. So that meant plenty of confrontation. One guy started yelling that I wasn't letting him in because he was gay and I was straight—which made no sense."

Shane K. went to Man's Country for the first time in 2013. "It was an eye-opening, transcendent experience. I loved it. It was a Thursday night, and I went back Friday and Saturday and Sunday. It wasn't crowded, but that gave me the chance to explore. I looked at the Etienne art. The first night I met two guys who were sort of friends and the three of us ended hanging out and having sex. Afterwards we talked for an hour. The next night they were there again, and again we had sex and then talked after. It was a situation where I would never be speaking to these two guys outside of these circumstances, and here we are having a fairly frank discussion about our lives. I had a lot of great conversations there. Once, I was walking around and this guy asked me if I wanted to have my ass eaten. I just said, no that's okay. He was sitting on the long-carpeted bench outside the orgy room. I eventually sat next to him and we talked for two hours. We had a candid discussion about gay sex and bathhouses and racism. He was a closeted black guy from Detroit. We talked about him and I told him a lot about myself. We were sitting there in towels— no clothing, no status indicators, nothing. We were two strangers hanging out and being completely honest with one another. He lived in Detroit so it wasn't likely we would see one another again, nothing sexual happened, but it was a fleeting connection that has stayed with me. Sometimes after sex, I would hang out with whomever I was with, and we would talk for a while. Doing that helped humanize anonymous sex for me. We still parted ways, but we at least shared a moment. That was important for me. I talked to a lot of guys there because many guys there were open to talking. That place brought out different people and it brought people together."

Shane K. continued. "I was okay with it being dirty. I sort of liked that. I liked that it felt a little dangerous, that was part of the appeal. That place had a lot of character. It had history. The men seemed more sexually adventurous there. I liked that more People of Color went there. There didn't seem to be any sort of body fascism there. It could be sketchy with the drugs. I saw plenty of drug use there, some really bad stuff—needles, an overdose, everything. The fact that it went on was part of being there. Those people and the drugs were a part of this world. Man's Country was a place to get your rocks off that gave me a sense of connection. I rarely felt connected in the gay community, but I felt connected there. I felt at home."

Despite the diminished business, Man's Country still had an iconic status in the community. Almost thirty years after his band, Knightklub, played the Music Hall on New Year's Eve 1985, Richard Knight, Jr. returned to shoot several scenes for *Scrooge & Marley*, which he co-wrote and co-directed. Man's Country served as multiple locations for the queer-themed variation of the Charles Dickens' classic, *A Christmas Carol. Scrooge & Marley* starred David Pevsner as Scrooge and Tim Kazurinsky as Marley. The cast included Rusty Schwimmer, Bruce Vilanch, Ronnie Kroell, and even Chuck in a cameo appearance.

"In our film," explained Knight, "the Ghost of Christmas Past zips 'Ben' Scrooge back to the 1970s (using poppers!). After being kicked out of home for being gay, Ben is discovered at an unnamed bathhouse by young Jake Marley. This scene was shot in the lobby of Man's Country and extras included patrons who were spending the day roaming the still open bathhouse…"

Actor David Pevser recalled shooting at the bathhouse. "When we were shooting in the lobby of Man's Country, where you pay to get in, actual patrons were coming in and looking at us like, 'What the fuck?'"

Scrooge & Marley also used the Music Hall for several scenes. The room was transformed to become the hottest gay club in town in a 1970s flashback. Knight continued, "Ben meets Bill, the love of his life, on the dance floor. I remember shooting a zillion takes trying to make 25 extras, all dressed in their 70s getups, look like 700. That definitely took some creative crowd placement. Though the extras went crazy practicing to 'Turn the Beat Around,' when it came time to shoot there wasn't any music, it was added later. Bruce Vilanch kept the entire cast and crew in stitches with his hilarious improvements to his lines. Everyone was warned to NOT sit on the carpeted stairs lined along the wall because we were afraid of what everyone would pick up!"

In the film, the Man's Country exterior was featured as well as one of the dressing rooms. The main staircase was used briefly, as was the stage. Knight explained, "The stage itself was used to recreate Purgatory and I remember the fog machines starting to fail just as the cameras were about to roll with Tim Kazurinsky and drag legend JoJo Baby. One last small scene showed Fezziwig [Vilanch] living in a men's hotel at Christmas. In our version, he was still filled with the holiday spirit, even after losing all his money. This was shot in one of those [rooms] that over the decades had probably seen a lot of action and, yes, there was a funky smell that was unmistakable. You know what smell I mean! Bruce, being Bruce, was a trouper and gamely squeezed into the [room] and we got the scene in one or two takes"

Knight added, "There was an air of grand decay to the place that was bittersweet and rather palpable. I recall during a break in one of the scenes gazing out over the dance floor and remembering the night I saw Divine whip the packed crowd into a frenzy. Glancing up at the stage I was lost for a moment in another reverie, catching a glimpse of myself nearly thirty years earlier, impossibly thin in my white tuxedo jacket, hair spiked up with gel and dangling ear clips trying to do the same on New Year's Eve 1985. Though I was never a patron in the traditional sense, I'm oddly warmed by having been a small part in the history of this iconic gay historical spot."

Edwin A. recalled that around 2014, Men's Room began having parties at Man's Country. Established in 2011, the purpose of the Men's Room was "to bring the old vanguard down to today' because so much of that world and that history was gone. Edwin A. attended three of the Men's Room parties at Man's Country. "They were dance parties—it was a great place to go get sweaty, and if you found someone you liked, you could take them downstairs and have fun. They had talent at those parties too. Lucy Stoole performed there, as well as Jezebel A. Gogo. The shows had a 1980s feel. The show part of those parties helped to give them the nostalgic feel they were going for."

The Fetish Tour, a sex-positive kink event, was held at Man's Country, as was the leather and kink event, the Rise of the Eagle. "They wanted to create an open kink and BDSM space because there was no place to really do it," added Dean Ogren. "That was the first time I played with Steve in public. I was worried about being judged, especially because there were going to be people there that I knew. I was in my head about it, but I ended up having a really good time. Once it started, I blocked out everything except the scene. People came up to me after and commented on how hot it was. That was so liberating, so exhilarating."

Man's Country also held a good deal of leather events and competitions. Ogren continued, "In 1992, I was in the Mr. Midwest Leather Contest which was held at Man's Country. At the time I didn't know what I was doing, but it was empowering. Later, I helped put on several leather shows at Man's Country. Pantheon of Leather was there as well as several other contests."

An assortment of sex-positive and body-positive groups had regular events and meetings at Man's Country. The Windy City Gay Naturalists, celebrating all shapes and sizes of bodies, met at the bathhouse. As mentioned earlier, the private gay men's masturbation group, the Windy City Jacks, also met at Man's Country.

Another group that met at Man's Country was MAFIA, which stood for Mid-America Fists in Action. "We had parties there," said group President Israel Wright. "We set up four or five slings in the Music Hall and basically took over the area. The upstairs became a floor of fisters. We created different stations. The parties were also held so that anyone who had an interest [in fisting] could come and learn about it, so there was an educational component."

When filmmaker Henry Harris visited Man's Country in 2017, he did so because he was unsure how long the bathhouse was going to be around. "So I was walking around Man's Country and discovered the Music Hall. I was immediately in love with the room. It was dark except for the one spotlight on the disco ball in the middle of the room. It was sublime. I had this odd feeling of being scared and awestruck at the same time. I don't encounter that sensation often and I thought—I want to do something with this room. A couple years before, I started shooting 16mm short films—rolls of 100 feet, so approximately two minutes and forty seconds. Anyway, I shot these experimental shorts, and they sat in the can. I didn't know what to do with them but now I knew, I wanted to project the films there."

Harris praised Ehemann and especially Marino for their openness to the idea and their support in making it happen. "The showing was called, *Portico: Films for the Music Hall.* It was three short films. *Moon Ballad No. 1* was footage of an abandoned golf course in Lake Geneva. The second was *Minotaur*, and that was using a hand-held camera and walking around Montrose Harbor, giving this sense of cruising the space. In *Special Velvet Demo*, my mom sewed a blue velvet romper, so it was her walking around in it outside. All three films were ten minutes total. All three films were of the outdoors. I liked thinking of the screen in the Music Hall as a portal. That room felt so vast that I wanted to expand that vastness. People assumed I was going to show porn when I talked about showing movies there [at Man's Country], but I wanted to use the outdoor scenes to expand upon the vastness of that space."

The screening was over November 2nd and 3rd, 2017. Harris recounted the event. "Marino helped with sound as well, so I could turn off the disco in the Music Hall and play outdoor sounds to go with the outdoor theme of my films. I was in the projection booth and played the combined movies maybe four or five times throughout the night. I was grateful for the space to show my work. At the time much of what I was seeing in galleries and museums seemed predictable and safe. I wanted to go outside these places, to somewhere less predictable with a less defined audience. After the last showing of the films, my soundtrack switched back to disco and a guy who had been sitting in the shadows clapped his hands and said, *Finally*."

Duke is one of a very few who worked at Bistro Too, the Eagle, and at Man's Country. "All three—I worked taking those places apart and I worked putting them together. The building was a big part of my life. This place helped me to define who I am."

"The last time I walked around the place," said Jon Krongaard. "I felt so strange, but so comfortable. That's why it survived all these years. Sure, it could be sketchy, but Man's Country was a comfort. No matter what was going on in the outside world, this other place was here for rent six hours at a time. It had changed and yet it really didn't. Behind these walls guys could have the fun they needed to have, do what they needed to do, and then go about their business. That freedom meant something."

"When Chuck took me on a tour of the place," said Mike Gifford. "It was like we were looking at two different things. He was describing what he was showing me, but the way it was years ago. By the way he was talking about it, Chuck did not see that Man's Country wasn't just run down—it was falling apart. I wanted to experience the place before it was gone. I had the room to the left at the top of the stairs. It took a minute to get the light because the dimmer had fallen off and just the metal prong was sticking out. The ceiling was dusty chicken wire. If you shook it, globs of dust would fall on you. The mattress as ratty and thin—like from a Victorian prison. At the end of the bed was a dent in the wall where the paint was worn away from so many people hitting their head while getting fucked. That was the sort of thing I loved about the place. My discovery of the day was the orgy room. There was an old porn playing and in front of it was a church pew. It was dark in there, so I moved closer. There was so much sperm on that pew it looked like it was preserved in amber. Sperm was covering the whole thing like all these tear drops."

"The last time I went there," said David Rustile. "I ran into Chuck. He was heading for his office and using a walker, but he gave me this really sweet smile. I remember seeing Chuck and his health on the decline and seeing Man's Country was doing the same. I couldn't help but think that it was the end of an era."

Chapter Thirteen

In October 2016, Chuck gathered his employees to make an announcement. He was selling Man's Country. A week later, Chuck stated in the *Windy City Times*. "The place is holding its own, but it is just getting to be too much for me." At 87, Chuck still came to work three days a week. "That's something I will miss. I don't know what I'm going to do with myself." When Chuck discussed the sale of the building, he joked that they'll probably tear it down and put in condos. "Land is premium in Andersonville and Man's Country occupies a lot of land." Indeed, the Man's Country complex occupied 20,000 sq. feet and had 113 feet of street frontage. In the interview, Chuck said the memories would make leaving Man's Country difficult. "Back in its heyday, it was something. One time I did a survey and asked our members why they came to Man's Country, only 20% said for the sex. A large part of the rest came to see the shows and have fun and to be with other gay men. Being with each other, that's what was so much fun.

"The Leather Archives and Museum were scheduled to come and remove some of the erotic artwork, like the pieces by Etienne, the Kris Studio photo prints, assorted statuary, and maybe an iconic sign or two. Renslow said that whatever the museum wanted, he was happy to give. "Except for one thing." Renslow nodded towards the large teak elephant statue in the lobby. "That's something they can't have. That is something that will be going with me." (Keehnen, *Windy City Times*, 2016).

In failing health for several months, legendary leatherman and community pioneer Chuck Renslow died on June 29, 2017 at the age of 87. Soon after his passing, the 5015 N. Clark St. property, known as Man's Country, was sold. The complex was demolished to make way for condominiums, just as Chuck had predicted.

In a *Chicago Tribune* piece, Ehemann said, "As bathouses go, it's not that the age of bathhouses is over, but the age of these gigantic bathhouses is probably over. The building is just really, really large. The upkeep has gotten expensive. Real estate taxes is what really killed Man's Country." (Bill Daley, *Chicago Tribune*, December 2017)

Once the paperwork for the sale was final, the only thing that remained after all those years was to have one big final event. The bash was called Loose Ends: The Man's Country Chicago Closing Party. The most notable thing about the party was that it wasn't just men, but women as well. According to promotional materials for the event, the Loose Ends party was held to celebrate "... the life of the historic gay bathhouse by welcoming all genders and gender non-conformists to a thirteen-hour disco party with full access to all three floors." The Loose Ends party began at eleven on New Year's Eve and ended on January 1st at noon. The party featured performances by Coco Iman, Toyota Corona, the Vixen Tony, Lucy Stoole, and more.

"We had a test run in October," said Marino. "We did a Halloween party that was open to everyone, and it turned out pretty well. I wish we had done this sort of thing earlier. The Loose Ends party was two months later. Everyone was there—gay, straight, bi, drag, everyone. Hundreds of people turned out. The place was full. We had four or five DJs and the party went all night. That night I saw straight couples fucking, gay couples fucking, lesbian couples. Everyone got along. There was not one problem all night."

"People who came to that really went all out—it was like a final bacchanal," said Dean Ogren. "There was a big crowd, so I'm glad it went out with a bang and we got a chance to leave our DNA there one last time."

In a 2017 piece by Aaron Gettinger in *The Advocate*, Ehemann said of the event, "This felt like a real bathhouse party, the first one at Man's Country in at least a decade. People got naked and occupied every part of the club." Ehemann added, "It's been a hell of a run, but my whole life with Chuck Renslow was a hell of a run. This club was definitely Chuck Renslow. He built it. It came out of his imagination. That concept, the big playground, that was Chuck Renslow. It was his sex drive, which was astronomical and insatiable. My only regret is that Chuck wasn't here for it. He would have loved it. He would have loved that there were women, but mostly he would have loved that it was not a rave. It was a true bathhouse party."

An enormous sale was held to sell off many of the Man's Country contents. "Lockers sold in blocks of six," said Mike Gifford. "Those were a hot item. There were keys, the key rack, lights, the membership cards."

"I bought twelve lockers," said Skip. "And a bag of sheets. Those sheets were bags of twenty for five dollars. An entire room was filled with them. Someone bought the door to Room 69. There were a lot of leftover prizes from raffles, so things like packaged dildos and Flesh Jacks and butt plugs, cock rings—that sort of thing."

Marino added. "The front gates, the bars on the windows, the murals in the staircase to the Music Hall with the guys climbing the stairs. Those were painted on plywood and some guy bought all of those and put them on the ceiling of his house. People wanted a lot of different things."

"The most surprising thing to sell was probably the glory holes," said Ron Ehemann. "I did not expect someone to come in and cut those out. We had someone buy the shingles on the wall in Chuck's office and was putting Post-its on them so they would be recreated exactly. A couple of people bought the doors of specific rooms. Lots of tools and towels and sets of sheets. The bars on the SM room, the slings, and the St. Andrew's Cross. The most expensive thing didn't sell, that was a four-by-eight-foot mural of our logo that ended up at the Leather Archives and Museum."

Chapter Fourteen

Though advertised as the final hurrah, the Loose Ends party was not the very end. A couple of weeks later, Ehemann emailed several people and asked them to meet him at Man's Country on January 16th. A couple dozen people were in attendance. I was among those gathered in the husk of the Music Hall. Almost everything had been stripped from the room. The heat and electricity had been shut off. Standing there in the darkness, it was cold enough inside to see your breath. We kept our coats on and used flashlights.

Ehemann was turning over the keys the next day. Ron spoke of the long history of the place, his personal connection to Man's Country, and what it meant to see it go. After he finished speaking, Ron passed out lists and shopping bags. We were having a scavenger hunt. Nowhere in the great Man's Country compound was off limits—even places typically marked Employees Only or Keep Out. Ehemenn told us to feel free to take whatever remained. "Whatever you don't take is just going to go." Flashlight beams cut the darkness as the group split apart in search of the items on our lists.

By then most of the contents had been donated or sold. The DJ and control booth were empty. The backstage area had been stripped as well, littered with nothing but the debris of decades. The hallways were pitch black. Flashlight beams cut the darkness—illuminating so many areas and rooms, such a history of pleasure. Man's Country was empty and yet felt fully occupied by its past.

"The scavenger hunt was fun," said Dean Ogren. "But I remember going around there with the flashlight and this place that had once seemed so enormous to me didn't seem that big anymore. Maybe I just grew up— Man's Country was definitely a part of that."

"That night I handed everyone present a small elephant with a black ribbon on it and said you can either take this with you or leave it in the building," said Phillip Bernal. While the scavenger hunt was in progress, Bernal was smudging the space with sage, clearing the area of trapped spirits, and blessing the space. Bernal explained. "There were people who had died there. There were a handful of spirits there that were very angry. There was that short hallway at the top of the stairs going to the second floor, the one that was a dead end—there was a lot of bad energy there. Some trapped energy in the DJ booth. The worst was at the entrance to the steam room. When I did that, I was hit with a huge sense of dread and evil. The feeling was so strong it sacred me." When asked what he told the spirits, Bernal explained. "They don't want to move on. As I was smudging, I did my blessings and told these angry entities they had to go. They needed to leave because this place wasn't going to be there."

Over the years, the very structure of Man's Country itself has been changed, revamped, covered, demolished, and all states in between. Chuck had joked, "Someday when they tear it down they are going to be amazed."

"With the first swing of the wrecking ball," said Joey McDonald, "I thought, they're tearing down Dad's house."

Mike Gifford was there during the demolition. "It was so strange looking at the backside of the building and seeing the Music Hall in ruins. You could see what it was and how grand it had been." Gifford collected 100 bricks from the ruins. Giving several away and giving 90-plus of the bricks to Ron Ehemann. Once demolition began, there was an overwhelming demand for souvenir bricks. Man's Country, as well as Bistro Too and the Chicago Eagle had played a part in the lives of so many in the LGBTQ community. Ron had the bricks affixed with a gold alloy plate that read,

5015 N. Clark St. Chicago
Manscountry — Bistro Too
Chicago Eagle

The bricks became a means of raising funds for Lori Cannon and her ongoing work at Groceryland. A donation to the organization meant obtaining a bit of history. "The sale of the Man's Country bricks brought in close to $750," said Cannon. "Many were large donations from European IML guests who offered substantial money. Also, since the closing, grocery donations have been coming in regularly from those who never knew about us, until they came to buy the bricks."

During the sale of the building's contents, Adam from the Wooly Mammoth had asked Ron if he could carve out a glory hole. A week later, Mike Gifford saw the glory hole in the Andersonville curio store. After some finagling, Gifford purchased it.

"Man's Country was an important institution," said Gifford. "I was worried someone who didn't respect the history behind this glory hole would buy it as a joke." Gifford donated the glory hole to the Leather Archives and Museum. His donation contract to the museum stipulated that the glory hole be displayed with the dried sperm intact as well as the wad of gum stuck to the plywood beside the hole. Before making the donation, Gifford brought the artifact to Outspoken, the renowned LGBTQ personal history/story night at Sidetrack Bar. During his story, Gifford stood beside the glory hole. "I talked about my relationship with Chuck and how much our talks meant to me. I talked about this carved piece of plywood being more than it appeared. After I gave my speech, I was amazed how many people came up and said they may have used that glory hole. Some were kidding, but most were sincere. It made me feel good about my decision to donate it." Among the items Gifford donated to the LA&M was a leather flag he rescued from the Man's Country ruins, "I remember right where it was, hanging in the back by the glory holes." However, the prize item Gifford managed to salvage was one of the glass blocks from the interior wall by the locker room. "That I keep on display in my living room."

On May 19th, 2018, less than a year after his passing, the portion of Clark Street south of Winnemac and north of Ainslie, where Man's Country bathhouse had stood, was given the street sign, Honorary Chuck Renslow Way. Over 100 folks joined Ehemann, including the Renslow family of friends, lovers, staff, and members of the leather and LGBTQ communities turned out to see Chuck honored as a visionary and a community leader.

Man's Country was the site of sexual exploration and celebration for forty-five years and several generations of gay men. Though its original grandeur had tarnished in later years, the impact of Man's Country, as well as Bistro Too and the Chicago Eagle, on the evolution of gay life in Chicago cannot be overemphasized.

The epidemic devastated bathhouse culture. The tubs were called sex dens, and the grand world they had created was simplified and demonized as dirty. Instead of being seen as sexual palaces of liberation, bathhouses became a dirty secret. Swept away was the venue for talent, the showcase for art, cultural centers, and places of sexual health and education. There also seemed an utter disregard for the role of bathhouses as social centers and the fact that, for many, connection and not sex was often the endgame.

"A common misconception is that people come here just for sex," said Chuck, "and that's not true. A lot of people come here just to be with their own kinds of people. Birds of a feather flock together. Lovers come here, just because they enjoy the atmosphere, they enjoy the strippers. They don't necessarily want sex. If they want it, it's available, yeah they'll grab it, but they're really here to be with people of their own kind." (*Leatherman,* 2011).

Although the walls of Man's Country have fallen and the building may be gone, some of that complex and magical world, the legend of Man's Country, will endure. Chuck always said he wanted Man's Country to be more than simply a bathhouse, and it was—much more.

Man's Country demolition. Photo: Ron Ehemann.

Acknowledgments

Thanks to the Leather Archives and Museum for being an invaluable resource in my research and for helping to make this project a reality. I would like to add a special thanks to Mel Leverich for her assistance in this book since day one.

Thank you to Gerber Hart Library and Archives for being a place that celebrates Chicago LGBTQ history and for always having the answer.

Big thanks to Ron and Gary. This book was made possible because you two knew so much of the story. Thanks for your time, insights, and images.

Thanks to all the dozens of forthcoming folks interviewed for this project. Thank you to everyone who shared memories as well as those who permitted use of their images. Without each of you the story would be incomplete.

Thank you to Ian and Sukie of Rattling Good Yarns Press. Thank you for the books you give to the world. Thank you for the care you take with me and for giving my work a platform.

Thank you to Tracy Baim. None of this would have happened without you.

Thank you to my husband Carl, for his patience, understanding, and for teaching me what love is all about.

Most of all, thank you Chuck. You were the inspiration behind this project. I said one day I would do it. I only hope that I did Man's Country justice.

About the Author

Owen Keehnen is the author of several fiction and non-fiction books including *Watch Me, Dugan's Bistro* and *The Legend of the Bearded Lady*, *Night Visitors, Jim Flint: The Boy from Peoria*, and *Leatherman: The Legend of Chuck Renslow*. Keehnen has also co-edited several books, including three volumes of the *Tell Me About It* series with St Sukie de la Croix. For several years, the queer writer and historian has been involved in preserving the LGBTQ history of the Belmont Rocks. Keehnen is also the cofounder of the LGBTQ education/history organization, the Legacy Project. He was inducted into the Chicago LGBTQ Hall of Fame in 2011. He lives in Chicago with his husband Carl and their dogs, Vince and Daisy

The author, Owen Keehnen, in the Man's Country phone booth tagged with fluorescent graffiti in the style of artist Keith Haring. Author's collection.

Made in the USA
Las Vegas, NV
30 October 2023

79941973R00090